# LOOKING BACK FROM THE NINETIES

# Looking Back
# from the Nineties

*An autobiography*

## Cicely McCall

GLIDDON BOOKS
NORWICH, NORFOLK

First published in 1994

© Cicely McCall

ISBN 0 947893 32 6

Published by Gliddon Books, The Reading Room,
79 The Street, Brooke, Norwich, NR15 1JT.


Printed by Antony Rowe, Chippenham, Wiltshire.

# DEDICATION

*To my great niece, Mary Ann Wingfield,*
*who first suggested writing this book.*


*To Harry and Bridget Oppenheimer, my niece,*
*who made it possible.*


*To my nephew Hilary McCall for unfailing support.*


*And to the many friends without whose encouragement this*
*book would never have been finished.*

# CONTENTS

LIST OF ILLUSTRATIONS

*(between pages 60 and 61)*

# PREFACE

The story of Cicely McCall's long and remarkable life is a wonderful example of an independent woman with strong personal convictions and pioneering social concerns. It is also a history of an era.

In this delightfully modest and witty autobiography, Miss McCall begins in 1904 with her childhood as the daughter of an affluent London family that suddenly lost its wealth. She takes us all the way to her later years as the feisty and resourceful restorer of her home, part of a fifteenth-century estate where, today, at age ninety-three, she lives and gardens happily. In the years between, she was expelled from Oxford for an absurd infraction of the rules; served as governess on the vast estate of a Polish noble family whose "peasants" starved on potatoes as they themselves entertained lavishly at banquets and shooting parties; established a shelter in Cairo for young women who had been sold into prostitution; became one of England's first psychiatric social workers and served as a headmistress and teacher at two prisons for young women; and pioneered the use of group homes for recovering mental patients. Her accomplishments earned her recognition by the Queen, and she was designated a Member of the British Empire (M.B.E.) in 1973.

McCall's no-nonsense descriptions of her struggles to earn a living and make her own way are absorbing and enlightening. What emerges is a truly engaging account of social history and a life that contributed greatly to its making.

– The Editor

1

# CHAPTER 1

# Childhood and Family Life

In 1904, when I was four years old, I developed appendicitis. We were on holiday at our country house, The Knoll, in Walmer, Kent, and the new young general practitioner told my father the only chance of my living was an operation by the famous surgeon, Sir Watson Cheyne. He happened to be at that time at Walmer Castle attending Lady Curzon (wife of the former Viceroy), who was recovering from appendicitis. Lady Curzon was so dependent on Sir Watson that she insisted on his sleeping at the castle and being in constant attendance. My father wrote to Lord Curzon to ask if the surgeon could be given sufficient time off to perform an operation on a small child living a half mile away. Permission was given and the operation was performed on our dining room table, presumably after breakfast had been cleared away.

I don't remember any professional nurses, but my mother and my nurse, Wake, looked after me. Wake had been my brother Geoffrey's nurse and before that maid to my grandmother. I suppose I had peritonitis, as the wound was kept open with a drain and was dressed every day. This was agony. I lay screaming, holding Wake's hand on one side and my mother's on the other. Both looked terribly distressed and I felt I ought not to be screaming. After all, I was four! But I could not stop. The calm voice of Dr. Smith droned on as he put on the dressings.

3

"Now here is the sheet. Here is the blanket. This is the eiderdown, and now we are all tucked up."

It was over for the day. No stitches were made and eventually the wound healed. The surgeon's fee was 100 guineas, an exorbitant fee in those days.

During my illness the gravel road past The Knoll was covered with straw to deaden the noise of horse traffic and the occasional car. Lady Curzon sent me a doll which my sister Nita christened Daisy Leiter after Lady Curzon's sister.I thought the doll's name was "Lighter," like the lamp lighter I could watch going down the street past our house in London. Lady Curzon also gave me a multi-coloured cock, christened George Nathaniel after Lord Curzon, and much loved. The gifts were brought by Lady Curzon's two hospital nurses, and I remember the veils and long cloaks they wore. I thought they were nuns and was terrified, for my Protestant nurse had told me blood-curdling tales of convents and I thought the "nuns" had come to take me away. There was a convent just up the road. But George Nathaniel was a comfort.

I had a happy, secure childhood with every comfort, presided over by parents who adored each other and dearly loved their children. Our family used to move from London to Walmer every Christmas, Easter and Whitsun and then for two glorious months in the summer. The routine was that my parents and I and one or two other members of the family – we were four boys and three girls – went by car. It took all day. We had a picnic, usually sitting under a tree on the grass bank at Leeds Castle, Kent. Our chauffeur, Chamberlain, had a separate picnic basket and sat under another tree. On the journey we nearly always had a puncture, sometimes two. Once the car caught fire and bags of flour from a conveniently placed baker's shop were poured on the smouldering engine and surprisingly put it out. I can't remember how we continued the journey but I don't remember going by train so I suppose we continued by car. I usually felt sick and had to be diverted by playing a game about the names of pubs we passed on the way.

When we got to The Knoll, Chamberlain and his wife and one or two children lodged in The Knoll Cottage with Milligan, the gardener and his wife. We also had Plum, the odd-job man who cleaned the boots and the silver and led the pony who drew the roller to maintain the croquet and tennis lawns. I don't know where the pony came from. He just appeared. There were also two housemaids, two cooks and a parlour maid, Blackman. It was her third job. I think she was paid £12 a year, and many years later she told me with pride that my mother was the first employer she had had who supplied a uniform. Before she came to us her mother made her uniform and presumably she got even lower wages.

As a small child I thought The Knoll, an undistinguished Victorian house, was the perfect holiday home. The grounds were large enough for tennis and croquet, for a few hens and for Father's clock golf and bowls and a large rose garden. On the other side of the main road there was a walled kitchen garden, now the site of three houses. The Knoll later became a nursing home. Somehow my brothers' school friends and later girlfriends all fitted in, and there was always room for our impoverished Irish relatives.

The servants slept somewhere in the attics, and three of my brothers occupied another attic bedroom. My youngest brother Geoffrey and I and Wake, our nurse, slept in the nursery. At our house in London there was a complete nursery floor, but at The Knoll Geoffrey and I used the window ledge (immensely wide in my memory) as our play space and Geoffrey's carpenter's bench. Later he spent all day and every day with the long-suffering Chamberlain in the garage. Father bought Geoffrey a lathe. When he was

5

fifteen, Father bought him a motorbike in pieces and told him to put it together. Which he did and it worked!

My eldest brother Hugh and my eldest sister Olive both married in 1908, Olive in January and Hugh in September. Hugh was in the Green Howards Regiment, which he joined during the South African war, after three years at Cambridge. Olive married Gerald Wollaston, who many years later became Garter King of Arms.

My brother Forster was also my godfather (my sister Nita and my mother were my godmothers) and of all my brothers he was the greatest tease. Quoting a current child's story book, "How Vain Jane became Plain Jane," the story of a little girl with long hair which she foolishly cut off, he christened me Jane, usually "Plain Jane" (and sometimes "Ugly" for short), although my long hair was not cut off. He would put me between his knees so that I could not move and say, "Now you are fixed." Knowing that there was nothing a little girl could do to free herself from a six-foot brother I made up a sentence which I thought sounded very grown up: "Not-for-ever-so-I-don't-mind."

The threat and the reply were repeated again and again. He never grew tired of it.

Maurice, my third brother, was perhaps the best-looking in the family. With his red-gold hair and sparkling blue eyes he was everyone's darling. He worked for a timber merchant and lived at home until he married. He went out dancing every night, or so it seemed, and as a child sitting half-way down the stairs in the morning after breakfast, I used to watch him put on his top hat, slightly tilted, and go swinging out of the front door to his office, pin stripe trousers and all.

In the First World War Maurice was at the front in Flanders and one day he came home unexpectedly on a week's leave. I had just been given a gramophone, the first we had had, and I showed it to him delightedly and played the dance tunes he loved. But he sat slumped in one of the morning room armchairs and made no reply. I couldn't understand his indifference; it seemed very strange. Afterwards I learned that the trench which had been sheltering him had caved in. His companion died and he was badly bruised. His group also had been gassed. Maurice went back to France at the end of the week, still unsmiling. Seven years later, his London doctor diagnosed tuberculosis and recommended that he try the healing effects of Californian sunshine. Maurice and his wife and baby daughter decided to emigrate, but shortly after their arrival in America the local doctor found he had cancer of the liver. He died a few weeks later, at only twenty-nine. Perhaps his illness was not unconnected with his time in Flanders, added to which were the privations he and his regiment suffered in the ill-fated Archangel Expedition of 1918-19. Maurice won a military cross in this inconclusive and little-known expedition to support the White Russians against the Bolsheviks.

At one time three of my brothers and an Irish cousin were in the front line in France at the same time. Our cousin was killed at Ypres and Hugh was wounded in the leg. One day my mother said she felt something had happened to Geoffrey, who was in the Royal Flying Corps. So strong was her conviction that my father got in touch with the War Office (there was no Air Ministry) and an enquiry was sent to Geoffrey's commanding officer. The answer came back that he was safe, though shaken. He had gone up in an observation balloon at the request of a friend, "to see what it was like." The balloon had been hit by enemy fire and both young men, together with an army major, had to jump out in parachutes. It was Geoffrey's first parachuting experience, and somehow he landed safely, though hitting his head. His companions were

7

killed. Geoffrey's friend was Basil Hallam, well known on the music hall stage for his song, "I'm Gilbert the Filbert." He was a favourite of pre-war London society and a close friend of Lady Diana Cooper and of the royal family. He had been at school at Charterhouse with my brother Maurice and so had asked Maurice's younger brother to join him at the Mess and come up for a ride in the balloon afterwards. His parachute never opened.

Geoffrey, who as a little boy had learnt so much about engines from our chauffeur, Chamberlain, left school when he was nineteen and joined the Artists' Rifles with Maurice. It was August 1914, and he wanted to join the Royal Flying Corps, but they would only accept trained pilots and there were no vacancies at their training school. After a few weeks, Geoffrey was allowed to leave the Artists' Rifles and enroll in the civilian flying school at Brooklands, where my father paid for his flying lessons. He passed his pilot's test and he was accepted as a pilot in the Royal Flying Corps. During one of his first flights, his plane's engine failed, and he was forced to make a crash landing – in Kent, where he was then stationed. His C.O. congratulated him on coming down in the only field within reach large enough to make this possible, adding that as a reward for his skill he would be sent to active duty in France. Geoffrey had flown a total of thirteen and a-half hours, including dual control.

A few weeks later he and a fellow pilot set off from Farnham for St. Omer in two separate planes with open cockpits. Each had only a road map on his knees. They were told to follow the railway line to the coast where they could refuel their petrol tanks, as thirty miles (the Channel crossing) was about the limit in those days. Unfortunately Geoffrey's companion turned right where the railway line branched and found himself heading for Dorset. Geoffrey correctly turned left and came down safely near Dover, where he re-fuelled. His next hop took him across the Channel, where he again re-fuelled. The third hop landed him at St. Omer, his base for the next few months.

At the end of the war Geoffrey was a Squadron Leader and acting Wing Commander, in command of a school for fighters at Turnberry, Scotland. The Royal Flying Corps said they would confirm his promotion after his twenty-first birthday; it was against regulations to do so before he had reached this age. However, the Armistice intervened and he left the Air Force still a squadron leader. Father was later repaid by the Royal Flying Corps for his flying lessons.

Geoffrey's love of flying never dimmed. In 1939, still on the reserves, he helped fly out the six planes held by the British government in Malaysia. Unfortunately the orders were to fly them to Singapore. Geoffrey was among the last British citizens there to be evacuated, to South Africa, where he spent most of the Second World War.

In those pre-1914 days my sister Nita was a staunch feminist. She was encouraged in this by her future husband's family, the Corbetts. She and Adrian (always known as Ann) were engaged for seven years and only married when he was made a partner in his solicitors' firm. When she learnt (in about 1911) that there was to be a meeting in Middle Temple Hall on the subject of women's suffrage, and that my father was to be one of the speakers, she insisted that I should be taken along to attend with the family party. Before the meeting Nita told me rather crossly that Father was speaking against women's suffrage, explaining that he had been "bounced into" the occasion and "hadn't really given the subject much thought."

There were several elderly officials on the platform and an attractive young woman with bobbed hair, introduced as Rebecca West. This was of course many years before West became an author of a world-wide repute, mistress to

9

H. G. Wells and eventually a Dame of the British Empire. She was very self-composed, very articulate, very firm and yet polite and deferential to her elderly opponents. The event was particularly memorable because it was the first time in my life that I realised Father could be wrong. It came as a great shock. I had always assumed before that he was an authority on everything, yet here he was talking what seemed to be nonsense. I was surprised that the revelation of this dent in his infallibility made no difference to my affection for him. He was still my much loved father – the kindest of men, a doting parent and, among other things, a wonderful guide to children visiting places of historic interest.

Father was probably at the height of his legal career in the early years of the twentieth century. Leader of the Northern Circuit, he would spend several days at a time in Manchester. He always returned with a present for Mother and sweets for the younger members of the family. Sometimes he brought Mother a piece of jewellery or some china or silver. I remember when I was quite small overhearing my mother say to one of my sisters regretfully, "He's brought me *another* tea service." It was Crown Derby. I was deeply shocked at her ingratitude.

My father was the second son of a Lisburn linen merchant. After getting his degree at Trinity College, Dublin, he came over to London to join the English Bar and with him came his friend Robert MacSwinney – Bob – who was to become his brother-in-law. Robert MacSwinney's sister, Alice, would marry my father and my father's sister, Agnes McCall, would marry Robert MacSwinney. They had a double wedding in London in St. George's Church, Tufnell Park.

My father had no influential friends to help him. While legal briefs were in short supply, he kept himself through journalism, contributing regularly to Charles Dickens's paper, *All the Year Round*. As briefs started to materialise, he boasted that he doubled his income every year. Then he sent for Alice (my mother), and later he offered a home and a warm welcome to her widowed mother. My grandmother spent half her time with her daughter and half with her son, also now settled successfully in London and becoming a leading light on mining laws.

Perhaps this early success went to my father's head. Like many Irishmen he had a jaunty self-confidence. But one contemporary, a solicitor, shook his head and said McCall would surely go bankrupt if he continued living at the high standard he set for us. That friend eventually shot himself because he had a morbid fear, quite without foundation, of eventual impoverishment. No such doubt clouded my father's horizon. He invested in an insurance company and when he was warned it was an imprudent investment, he put more money into it. It failed and he lost heavily.

Father, I was told once, had been offered a Judgeship in Bombay but Mother had persuaded him to refuse as the boys were still at school. He always hoped for a Judgeship in London but it never came. Perhaps he was too Irish.

During the First World War there were successive cutbacks in our standard of living. The car was sold and Chamberlain, our kind chauffeur who had taught Geoffrey so much, left. In 1918 The Knoll was sold and two years later our London house in Lexham Gardens was sold. My parents moved temporarily into my elder sister's house in Barkston Gardens. Father's failing finances were never discussed in my hearing and I was puzzled at the changes.

One day I overheard my sister describing Father's admission that he did not have enough money to put down for the deposit on a flat they hoped to buy. My parents moved into a flat in Earls Court Square. Mother started rationing the whisky she poured daily into Father's decanters.

Father got a new job with a strange title, Registrar of the Railways and Canals. He still went to his chambers every day, but rather later than he used to. And every Sunday my parents and I went to the Temple Church, by underground now instead of car. We had lunch in the Middle Temple Hall with the Benchers.

In 1919 my father was awarded the K.C.V.O. He died in 1934.

All through the decline in Father's finances, Mother remained loyal and loving, and he thought as much of her when he was old as he had when, as a young man, still a bachelor, he had commissioned her miniature, now my most treasured possession. She wears bog oak earrings made in the shape of an Irish harp, and her red hair is piled high on her head. I was told that Father had had it painted when he was in London before they were married, and my mother's parents disapproved of his forwardness.

Luckily I can remember my mother's good looks, her red curls and her gaiety. I have a vivid picture of her at our house in Lexham Gardens on the night she was presenting her three prospective daughters-in-law at Court. She wore a blue dress and matching velvet train. Pinned into her hair was a diamond fan-shaped brooch holding the regulation white curled feathers. (I know my American sister-in-law to-be waited nervously in the hall but I can remember little about her or the other two.)

Mother swept down the stairs, head held high, blue eyes sparkling. Wake had brought me down from the nursery to see them off. Mrs. Watling, the cook, and the kitchen maid came up the basement stairs and stood in the passage with the rest of the staff. My brother Geoffrey, perhaps on holiday from his prep school, also remembers gazing up at Mother as she walked down the stairs, her train spread out behind her.

Did they all, with their feathers and trains, and Father in

his knee breeches, get into the family Standard to drive to Buckingham Palace? I can't remember.

Once a year, when our family still had money, Father used to visit Bath to drink the waters. Mother and I went too, and Father took me round the Roman wells. We visited Glastonbury, and bought a "Glastonbury thorn" which was planted at The Knoll and duly flowered at Christmas. We drove through Savernake Forest, a magical experience for a small girl. I think we stayed in lodgings. Where Chamberlain slept, I have no idea.

My mother was reserved and sometimes forbidding in her very correct behaviour, but she had flashes of sudden gaiety. Often in the evening she would sit at the piano and sing us Irish songs as she used to sing them in her old home in Galway, where she had been the soloist in the church choir. Her father had been a doctor and aside from Bob, who would come over to the English bar at the same time as my father, she had another brother who went to Australia to practise medicine. Her mother, determined that her three children should not be at a disadvantage when they went out in the world, taught them dancing and how to play bridge in spite of the strong disapproval of their stern doctor Father. Fortunately, he went to bed early, so the lessons were given in the evenings while he was out of the way.

My grandmother also taught her children French, and indeed she spoke fluent French herself even in her old age. In spite of her Protestant upbringing, she sent my mother to a French convent in Orleans when she was fifteen, accompanied on the journey by Bob, who was eighteen. My mother used to tell us how she had to have her bath in the convent wearing a nightgown to hide her nakedness. She travelled back to Galway by herself the next year and in Paris heard how her hostess had been forced to eat cooked rat during the "war."

13

All through my childhood we always had one or more dogs, usually acquired by one of my brothers and left behind when they went to the university or the army. Bess was my favourite. She was a Gordon setter and in London she would walk daily to Kensington Gardens with Wake and me. Occasionally, on Sunday after church, Father would join us, in top hat and carrying a rolled umbrella. On weekdays, Wake and I would feed the sparrows that waited for us just inside the side gate to the Gardens. Outside sat an old woman selling balloons.

I used to get 6d. a week pocket money. When I was already at day school I saved up to buy a Kodak No. 2, which took oblong photos, grander I thought, than the square ones taken by the No. 1 I had inherited from one of my brothers. Kodak No. 1 cost 5s. and the No. 2 (I thought), 7/6d. But when, after months of saving, I went to the shop I was told it cost 10s. and I only had 7/6d. No one suggested they would lend me the extra 2/6d. and sadly I had to make do with my old No. 1. Yet my parents were loving and generous, and at that time, rich. I suppose they thought it taught me something.

# CHAPTER 2

# Oxford

When they came back from their finishing schools in Hanover, both my sisters had stayed at home till they married. Nita, the younger of the two, spent seven years engaged to her future husband, Adrian Corbett, and during these seven years she sewed her trousseau. Every sheet, every pillow case, every tablecloth and towel was embroidered with their joint initials. My mother often referred with surprised approval to the fact that Nita's initials were combined with those of her future husband, an innovation which I think must have been inspired by Nita's more enlightened future in-laws. Normally only the husband's initials appeared.

Sitting in a low chair by the French windows in the morning room in our London home she plied her needle and linen thread every day except Sundays, from breakfast to lunch. Or so it seemed to me. To me she was a family fixture, like a piece of furniture. But she was also a much loved part of my life and clearly had given more than a little thought to the future of her younger sister.

Nita told me, to my surprise, that I would have to live a very different life from my sisters and earn my own living when I grew up. I did not know any female family friend who did this. True, a cousin had a hat shop off Sloane Square which she shared with a Russian refugee friend, but this was a family joke, not to be taken seriously; obviously

15

she did not *have* to do it. I did know two elderly cousins who had been to university, one a headmistress and one a doctor. But it was men who went to university and earned money, not women, I thought.

I don't think my mother ever discussed Oxford with me. It was Nita's idea and it was she, when I was about twelve, who took me to Oxford to see a family friend, a contemporary of my brother Geoffrey, and a student at Somerville. In the 1914 war Somerville College was housed in Oriel, and Somerville became a hospital.

Dorothy gave us tea in her room. She wore, much to my envy, a pink crêpe de chine blouse and a navy serge skirt. I was very impressed.

She told us about the rigours of men's colleges in war time and how she had to cross the quad after dark to get a bath. That is all I remember of Nita's efforts to introduce me to university life, except that she and her husband would generously pay my fees there in the future.

Francis Holland School, Graham Street, the fashionable, expensive school where I had gone at the age of eleven, did not cater for would-be university students. Nevertheless, it was decided that I was to prepare for university, and I found suddenly that my two-hour a day piano practise was cut out completely, while my Latin classes doubled and a newly appointed member of staff undertook to teach me Greek. No one else in the school learnt Greek. But Greek was compulsory at that time for university entrance.

It was only after Nita married and lived in Campden Hill, London, that I got to know her better. I used to visit her little house in Sheffield Terrace nearly every weekend. Those were the days when a small girl could walk unmolested through the streets of Kensington. Nita had no children for the first seven years of her marriage and I suppose I filled the gap.

16

On one occasion, however, the unexpected happened. When I first went to the Graham Street School I was driven in the family car by Chamberlain, rather to my embarrassment. Other children arrived by bus or tube. But after the car was given up I was allowed to go alone on the underground, a gratifying step up the ladder to independence.

Then one day, on the way to the Earls Court Station, I saw a man on the other side of the street exposing himself. Surprised and puzzled – he made no attempt to approach me – I later mentioned it to my mother. She was clearly horrified but made no comment. The next day, with no explanation, our nursery maid accompanied me. I was furious. It was an insult, I felt, to my new independence. Why couldn't I go alone like other girls? No reason was ever given.

I took "Smalls" (university entrance examinations) at Graham Street and failed, Greek and all. For my last year there, in 1917, I became a boarder and was made head girl. Boarders lived in a house in West Eaton Place. Our daily walk (in "crocodile") took us past Chelsea Barracks until the new war-time recruits started bayonet practise, all too realistically, just inside the iron railings bordering the pavement. They gave blood-curdling yells as they charged the stuffed sacks propped up on posts and we watched in horror. After that our daily walk was diverted.

It was decided that I should leave Graham Street and be sent to an Oxford coach, Mrs. Hunter, who lived in Banbury Road, Oxford and took a small number of girls working for university entrance. There, for the first time, I saw the possibilities of university life. Mrs. Hunter's establishment was tough, the food was awful, and the rooms were icy, but the educational standards expected and enforced were high and the enthusiasm was genuine.

When I arrived there were six or seven girls at Mrs.

Hunter's working for their university entrance. The one exception was a French girl, Odette, who had been brought over from Paris by her mother. In halting English her mother had asked about the daily routine. Mrs. Hunter replied that the morning was given over to coaching, the afternoons were free, and the evenings were spent in studying.

After Odette had been with us a week or two she asked in a puzzled voice, "When do we go coaching?" Indeed the domestic arrangements of the house were so Victorian that coaching would not have been at all out of place. Mrs. Hunter had a kindly shadowy husband somewhere in the background, and one small daughter who floated in and out of the house on her way to school, and hardly ever spoke, even at meal times.

Odette found the icy English house hard to bear. She used to sit in her bedroom crouching over a very small gas fire, wearing a warm woolly dressing gown on top of all her other clothes. None of the rest of us in our sparsely furnished rooms had any heating.

All the other students came from expensive schools which had never sent pupils to a university. We all failed our first attempt at entrance examinations. We all passed at our second, once Greek had ceased to be compulsory. Three of us were accepted at St. Hugh's College.

I had never visited Oxford before, except for the one visit to Dorothy at Oriel, and the beauty of the buildings and the enchantment of the River Cherwell captivated me. More important, I made friends there who have remained friends throughout my life.

Every Sunday, immediately after breakfast, my friend Liz and I would punt for miles up the river and not return till early evening. In those days there were strict regulations about women using the river. You had to prove you could swim, I think fifty yards, and produce a certificate to this effect before you could hire a boat. Every women's college insisted on this.

After the restrictions of school life and the rigours of Mrs. Hunter's establishment, life at St. Hugh's seemed too good to be true. The companionship was intoxicating. But the superficial education many of us had received at our previous schools caught up with us, and at the end of our first year, I and several others failed History Previous, our first-year examination. We all took it again the next term and all passed except for myself and one young woman who left to become a Froebel teacher. I returned home, went to a coach in London, re-took History Previous and passed. Then I returned to St. Hugh's for the summer term and was welcomed by other members of my year with a warmth I still remember gratefully.

There were in those days many college rules about social behaviour which today would be unbelievable. Stories of my classmates' late-night entries through ground-floor windows were common. I knew few men undergraduates, so such strictures did not affect me. But there was a rule that any woman student who went out with a man who was not a university student must inform a member of the staff. Permission was then automatic.

One such male friend came to take me out and through sheer idiotic inertia I did not inform a don before we left; I remember seeing the French tutor disappearing round a corner and thinking I ought to run after her and get permission, but while I hesitated she disappeared. Why bother, I thought, since permission is always automatic? I was wrong, for that tutor saw me on the river and reported me, and I was "gated" for the rest of the term. That meant no theatres – a nuisance but not a disaster.

One day later in the same term Liz had a visit from her elder sister, and the three of us, together with another girl

19

who was visiting Oxford, took a punt and a picnic and spent the whole hot summer Sunday together. Liz and I returned to college at six p.m. to attend Chapel, which was compulsory and was the official method of registering residence. We then went back to the river with our two visitors and returned to St. Hugh's at nine p.m., the hour at which the college gates were shut every night.

Before going back to the river I had gone to the college notice board hanging in the passage leading to Hall. Here students were required to sign a headed sheet of paper if they planned to be out till nine p.m. I could not find the usual sheet and imagined it had been forgotten. So I added Liz's name and mine to another posted list and noted on it that our names referred to the normal nine o'clock deadline.

Delighted with our having spent a wonderful day on the river, we hurried back in the evening but unfortunately cut it too fine. While Liz got to college as the clock struck nine, I was running up the garden path of No. 4 St. Margaret's Road, my residence, just as the parlour maid locked the front door. She let me in, but reported me.

The next morning at breakfast I sat next to my tutor, Miss Ady, who was head of No. 4. I told her of our lovely day on the river and as usual she grunted and nodded in her usual endearing but inarticulate way. I realised I might be blamed for causing the maid to retrace her steps and let me in, but felt it was hardly a matter for grave concern, and nothing was said.

After breakfast, I was summoned by Miss Jourdain, the Principal. Eleanor Jourdain was a strange character. A brilliant French scholar, she held a doctorate of Paris University and was a much valued university lecturer in Oxford. In 1911, she and her great friend Miss Moberly, who had been the previous Principal of St. Hugh's College, wrote An Adventure, an account of their visit to Versailles.

20

The book had a wide circulation, and I had read it before going to Oxford. Many students believed in Miss Jourdain's celebrated capacity for second sight, though some were skeptical. I remember once walking behind her in the corridor and wondering whether I should catch up with her to put some unimportant question about a college activity. As I had hesitated, Miss Jourdain turned round and said,

"Cicely, do you want to see me?"

It was uncanny. She had a disconcerting way of never looking you in the face when you talked to her, although I had always found her approachable.

Miss Jourdain was also a very good pianist. Late at night one would sometimes hear her playing strange melodies on her piano in her ground-floor sitting room.

Now I was about to hear why she had summoned me. I had broken a rule, she told me. I had been out late. I must be sent down – "rusticated" – for the rest of the term. I must leave that day. In vain I pointed out that I had written our names down on the board and that I had been only one minute late. It made no difference, said Miss Jourdain. I must leave Oxford.

I was shattered. I went back to No. 4, shut myself in the bathroom and sobbed.

Liz was summoned by Miss Jourdain.

She said afterwards that she had never before been spoken to by anyone with such venom and fury. She was "gated" for the rest of the term. Dumbfounded at Miss Jourdain's virulent attack, Liz explained that we had written down our names and that she had returned by nine o'clock. Her explanation was brushed aside.

Much later we discovered that students were in fact expected to stay in college on Sundays after the compulsory Chapel evensong. St. Hugh's is in North Oxford, not on the river bank, and perhaps not many students had our energy to bicycle back to college for Chapel and then back

21

to the river for a further hour or so before the final closing of the gates at nine p.m.; possibly this infringement of the rules had never before occurred. So while it was true that we had broken a rule, our signatures on the Hall notice-board were proof that we had done it in ignorance.

That evening, by a defiantly late train (maybe nine p.m.!) I returned home to London and told my parents the terrible news. My father was appalled. He went to see Miss Jourdain but she said I had broken a rule, no student was allowed out on Sunday after Chapel and that was that. He gave in.

Miss Ady, who had not been consulted by Miss Jourdain and to whom I had babbled so innocently at the breakfast table, also pleaded on my behalf. But to no avail. The Junior Common Room protested and the question was raised at the Council, to which my father made representations. Miss Jourdain replied it was a matter of internal discipline, not to be questioned.

I returned to St. Hugh's the next term very chastened. I was two terms behind the others and conscious of my failure. So, in consultation with my tutor, I changed course and read for a Pass Degree, which meant taking the first half of my Finals (now Pass Degree) the following term. Again I failed. All the joy of Oxford life had evaporated for me. I could not expect Nita and her husband to keep paying my fees when I was such a failure and I decided to give it up and come down.

A year later Miss Jourdain dismissed Miss Ady from her appointment as Vice-President of the College. Miss Ady was a university lecturer and a distinguished historian with a national reputation. All hell was let loose. It was called "The Great Row." Senior staff resigned. Letters of protest appeared in The Times. Students withdrew their applications for entrance. Questions were asked by university bodies as well as the College Council. St. Hugh's sank to an all-time low. Then suddenly, Miss Jourdain had a heart attack and died in the lavatory.

I wrote to Miss Ady and said I felt I might have been the innocent cause of her ruptured relations with Miss Jourdain. She replied in her usual affectionate terms that perhaps it might have been not unconnected.

I left Oxford feeling that what had happened was a failure too fantastic to explain to strangers. Sent down because you returned to college one minute past nine? Who would believe it? For years I never went back to Oxford and never volunteered that I had been there. I felt that the experience was a slur on my character that I could never live down and it left me with an inferiority complex about my intellectual and academic abilities from which I only recovered years later, when I won a £300 American Commonwealth Scholarship at the London School of Economics and subsequently gained a Mental Health Certificate.

With no qualifications and my self-confidence gone, I decided to take a secretarial course as the quickest way to become self-supporting. So I signed on at Mrs. Hoster's secretarial school, where nine months later I learnt shorthand and typing.

Then through my cousins the MacSwinneys, I was offered a job in Poland: to teach English to the four children of the Prince and Princess Olgierd Czartoriski. I was having problems in my private life, for my boyfriend had told me there was no chance of his making a living at the Bar (he later became a Q.C.) and therefore no chance of marriage in the foreseeable future. So he intended to take a teaching job in Japan.

Poland seemed to me as good a place as any to get away from it all.

# CHAPTER 3

# Poland and London

I travelled to Poznan via Berlin by train. It was autumn
1923. At the frontier there was a very thorough search of
my luggage. Every garment was unfolded and examined. A
packet of sanitary towels baffled the customs man and,
with no common language, explanations were impossible.
With a shake of his head he let them pass.

Then came the body search by a pleasant woman flanked
by an Alsatian guard dog. I was grateful that he was more
interested in his dinner than stray travellers, and the search
was soon done.

At Poznan I was met by H.R.H. Princess Marie Czartoriska, mother to Prince Olgierd Czartoriski. He had been in
touch with the British ambassador to find a suitable
English girl to teach his four children, and here I was. The
children's mother, H.R.H. Princess Mathilde Czartoriska,
was a niece of the old Emperor Francis Josef of Austria, a
Hapsburg. Old Princess Marie spoke no English and we
conversed in French. From Poznan, she and I took a train
to the station nearest to Sielec, the Czartoriski's home. We
were met there by a closed two-horse carriage.

Sielec was a rambling two-storey house set in a park
surrounded by pine plantations. Beyond the wide semi-
circular drive lay the stables, in one of which lived the
coachman. If he had a family, I never saw any sign of them.
The stable boys also slept with the horses. The cook, I was

told – a man – slept in the kitchen. I think the women staff slept in the attics, except for the German-speaking nurse and nursery maid, who slept with the children on the first floor.

I had a ground-floor bedroom and used the children's bathroom on the first floor. On my first morning I was startled to be woken by a young Polish maid, who retrieved my hand from under the duvet, kissed it and replaced it. Then she drew my curtains.

The Czartoriski children spoke a little French and German, but no English. They would come to my room for lessons, but most of the day they were with their Polish tutor or in the nursery. Their mother, Tildy, spoke English to them if I was present. I spent a lot of time with her and became very fond of her.

Sometimes Olgierd would take me out shooting. He drove a high gig and a coachman stood up behind. There were no boundaries to his driving and we would bump roughly over banks and career across ditches. He shot deer and anything else in sight. It was great fun if you held on tight.

In the summer the family moved to Baszków, another property, about ten miles away. We went by road in a variety of horse-drawn carriages; they had no car. Baszków was only habitable in summer as it had no heating. There the Czartoriskis would entertain six to eight guests for the early autumn shoot. At the end of three or four days' shooting, all the game was laid out in front of the stone steps leading up to the front door. Tarred torches would be lit at the corners and the stable staff and the gamekeepers would stand around in the shadows. Then in the evening after dinner, all the guests would troop down the stone steps and examine the carcasses: birds, foxes, deer, or whatever.

I used to ride a young horse there, which was well

25

beyond my capabilities. One day, galloping across a field, he shied at a ditch and sidestepped into a plot which I later learnt belonged to a peasant. (I had thought everything in sight belonged to the Prince.) The owner suddenly appeared from nowhere, a scythe across his shoulder. I spoke no Polish and couldn't understand his threats, but my one Polish word, *Angelka*, (English girl) stopped him in his tracks, and soon other farm workers appeared and confirmed my exotic status. When I told Tildy she was alarmed and afterwards sent a groom with me. When we returned to Sielec my rides stopped.

On Ascension Day, in a kind of thanksgiving ceremony from tenants to landlord, the family was visited by a delegation from the village. Small girls and boys carried plates covered with flowers and on some sat a pigeon – whether doped or tied down I never discovered, but it was immobile. These were presented to the Prince and then carried off by retainers.

The Czartoriski children were Konstanty (nine), Cilla (eight), Isa (six) and little Leszek (four). We – the four children, the nurse, the nursemaid, and I – used to go out for regular walks. The children's favourite was by the railway line, where we could shout and wave at the trains. One day Princess Marie, the children and I were being driven through the forest in a two-horse carriage. There was snow on the ground and the forest was dark and forbidding. The children were amusing themselves by picking branches off the pine trees and sticking them into the carriage windows. Suddenly the old coachman fell off his box. The horses stopped and reared up. We could not immediately open the windows or doors as they were stuck with bits of pine. At last I got out and found the coachman, very drunk, under the horses' hooves. I managed to seize their bridles and to my surprise, both horses calmed down and the coachman crawled out,

26

somewhat battered, and climbed back on to his box. Princess Marie was unwilling to continue and so we walked a short way to the nearest cottage and somehow a message was sent back to ask for alternative transport. Another carriage arrived in due course, and, followed by the drunken coachman, now sober and tearful, we returned home. Tildy's only comment was that she knew an English girl would know what to do. I still remember the cottage woman, who told Princess Marie that she and her children lived on potatoes only, and that now they too were getting short.

The family had a German Shepherd dog, Luks, black and tan and very shaggy, as well as a number of horses. When the young colts were brought out for inspection they were made to gallop round the great circular drive and we watched from the front of the house. Luks would chase them and snap at their heels. One day he got kicked and limped back, one eye hanging out. Tildy, in the surprisingly insensitive way which sometimes startled me, laughed. No one did anything about it. Luks stood still, quivering. I took him away and bathed the eye socket. The eye was lost. From that moment, he became my constant companion. He followed me everywhere and practically lived under my bedroom writing table.

In the evenings we all had dinner together. If there were guests it was very grand, with five or six courses and lots of drink, and the children absent. If there were no visitors it was not grand at all: two sardines and a baked potato for each of us, with nothing more.

I went on two holiday trips with Tildy, once to St. Raphael, France, where we spent happy hours walking around the flower market and coming home with a great bargain, an entire armful of mixed carnations. Tildy also took me to Monte Carlo because she said I ought to see the gambling, of which she disapproved. Olgierd, she

27

said, enjoyed it. Encouraged by Tildy I had my long hair "bobbed," which Tildy thought highly entertaining.

Once we went for a weekend to what was then called Danzig, now Gdansk. When we reached the station for the return journey I was told my passport was out of date and that I would not be allowed to travel. Tildy showed very little concern, merely saying that an English girl would always sort things out, and that no doubt the British Consul would arrange something. With that, she left for home. It was Sunday and the Consulate was closed. At my hotel, to which I returned alone to telephone, I got little sympathy. The Consul told me that emergency visas were issued only in cases of death. I replied that I had little money, knew no one in Danzig, could not pay my extended hotel bill and that my employer had returned home. Very reluctantly he lent me the necessary money and provided the visa. When I got back to Sielec Tildy said only, "I knew you'd manage."

Tildy and Olgierd made a yearly visit to Paris, where she kept some of her jewellery in a Paris bank. Was it for security? In Poland she seldom wore much jewellery, even at the family's grand dinner parties.

Sometimes they would stay with friends, with General Carton de Wiart or with one of the Potocki families. Once Tildy told me that at (I think) Llanciut, Olgierd had a bedroom located down another corridor, some distance from hers. She was surprised, and whether Olgierd was pleased I don't know. Apparently, swapping partners was taken for granted in this company, but not by Tildy.

At the Baszków shoots, I remember one guest, Countess X, arriving in her Rolls. She was considered a good shot; none of the other women had guns and most of the guests were men. Here is an excerpt from a letter I wrote Nita on July 27, 1925:

Baszków
Powiat krotoszynski
Stac. kol. Zduny lub Kobylin

....The other day I saw the "Kontusz," the Polish
national dress, which used to be worn always by the
aristocracy, and after the partitions was allowed only
by the Austrian court. Now Poland is free no one
apparently dares wear it at all because of the socialists!
But today there was to be a Czartoryski wedding in
Warsaw and the whole family had orders to put on all
their war paint. Prince Olgierd tried on his to show
me. On top he wears a great big white coat, trimmed
with sable, and an enormous sable cap, almost as big
as a guard's bear-skin, with a great diamond brooch
and an osprey like a blooming Maharajah. You only
wear the coat on your shoulders, to be slipped off at a
moment's notice. Underneath he had a red, tight-
fitting coat, also unbuttoned and also with sleeves
which you didn't wear. It came to his knees and below
were red cloth breeches to match – rather like "plus –
fours" and tucked into bright yellow boots. These
sleeves were slit all the way down and could be crossed
at the back and hooked together. Underneath that
was a high-necked, gold brocade tunic, and wrapped
nine times round his middle a red and gold sash, with
the ends hanging down at one side. The sashes are just
the loveliest things. He has three sashes, and before
the war they cost £100 a piece. Another Czartoryski
has his set with emeralds. All of them are made in four
colours, two on each side. You fold them down the
middle, so as to show only one colour, except for the
ends. They are generally gold tissue or gold brocade.

When I had been with the Czartoriskis for nearly two

29

years, my brother Geoffrey wrote to ask me to join him in Calcutta. Fond as I was of Tildy and her family, I did not want to spend the rest of my life in Poland and so, with regret on both sides, I left.

I knew that Father had invested for me £200, a legacy which a family friend had left to me some twenty years previously. This, I thought, would pay for my fare to India, with some left over. In my ignorance I thought that it must have increased in twenty years. But when Father repaid me, the sum had inexplicably become £180. Nevertheless, it paid for my fare.

For a year I kept house for Geoffrey. We visited Agra and Delhi, an unforgettable experience. I danced and played tennis. Then it seemed time to take life more seriously and I returned to London.

Liz, my never failing friend, got me a job working as a sales girl in a knitwear shop in London called "Mary Brown." The owner had been governess to Liz and her sisters many years earlier. I lived at home and earned £2 a week. Part of my duties was to act as a model, something for which I had had no training nor knowledge. I mentioned this casually to my mother one day and said there was to be a dress show the following week. She made no comment. But that day, when I walked into the shop from the changing room, there, to my astonishment and consternation, sat my mother and Nita in the front row. I was wearing a long pale blue evening dress, chosen probably because of my red hair, and fortunately someone sitting next to my family made a complimentary remark. Mother left before I was free to talk to her, but Nita told me that Mother, who had been deeply shocked about my modelling, was reassured that I was not doing anything positively immoral. The visit was never referred to again.

Customers at the shop were usually kind to my ignorance

and shyness, and the other, older assistant was most supportive and tolerant. Mary Brown herself could not have been kinder.

There was no chance of promotion at Mary Brown's and when I heard of a vacancy at Gabbitas Thring, the scholastic agency, I applied. I was told that the senior member of staff was likely to retire in the not too distant future. This proved untrue. Nevertheless I spent two years in their tiny dark offices in Sackville Street and learnt a lot about public and private schools. I was earning better pay, £168 a year, and when this was raised to £200, this enabled me to pay for a holiday in France and later a London flat of my own. Meanwhile, I economised on fares by walking to the office every day from Manchester Square, where I rented a room. At midday I walked up Regent Street to Cavendish Square where I lunched at the Cowdray Club of which I was a member. Lunch consisted of a Ryvita biscuit and cheese, an apple and a cup of coffee. It cost ten pence. These economies also enabled me, on rare occasions, to take a taxi in the evening if I dined out. Theatres were usually paid for by someone else. Clothes I usually made myself.

My job at Gabbitas Thring ended when, lying in bed recovering from a severe bout of flu, I came to the conclusion that there was no promotion for me in the foreseeable future, and I gave in my notice. An agency sent me particulars of a vacancy with a far better salary and the enticing prospect of living in Egypt. So began three years under very different circumstances in Cairo. It was 1926.

# CHAPTER 4

# Egypt

The job in Cairo was with the International Bureau for the Suppression of Traffic in Women and Children. They wanted someone over thirty, with fluent French and a knowledge of committee procedure. The successful applicant would do education work in Cairo, Alexandria and Port Said, and supervise the work of the bureau's shelter in Cairo. The salary was £300, nearly half as much again as I was getting as assistant in Gabbitas Thring. I had no knowledge of committee work. I was twenty-six. But I did speak French and I liked the idea of living in Egypt. I applied. To my surprise I was given an interview and accepted on condition I did three months training in the bureau's London office. There I read reports and relevant documents, I was interviewed by the Home Office (why I never knew) and was told that on my way to Cairo I must spend a few days with Sister Margaret Clare, who lived in the south of France and had worked in Cairo for some twenty years.

Sister Margaret was a remarkable woman. She had belonged to an Anglican order which she had left, some said because she was diagnosed as having tuberculosis and some said because she had a disagreement with the order. However it was, she continued to wear a grey habit and veil. Five foot nothing, she had a sparkling sense of humour and unlimited courage. In Cairo she had trudged the back streets, unmindful of riots, and had visited brothels and the government inspection centres charged with examining registered prostitutes for venereal disease on a weekly basis. Though she could do nothing about the nefarious regulation system, which "regulated" only a fraction of the actual number of working prostitutes and was powerless to detect the disease they so skillfully concealed, she had fearlessly tackled brothel keepers and pimps who imported young prostitutes, and she had in many cases arranged for their return to their own European countries of origin.

On arriving at Sister Margaret's little house on the French Riviera, which she shared with a retired hospital matron, also from Cairo, I found she had prepared notes for me on all the leading officials and civil servants in Cairo with whom I might have dealings. They were vivid thumbnail sketches, always lively, often libellous. I was told to keep the notes under lock and key, and I did. Sister Margaret explained the role of the police, led at that time by English officers, and also the curious Courts of Justice ("Capitulations"), one to represent each of the many nationalities living in Egypt at the time. At the head of it all was His Excellency, the British High Commissioner and his bevy of officials, as Egypt was still a British protectorate.

On arrival in Cairo I was given lodgings (a bedroom) in the Bureau's shelter. As I was being shown round, I was told that no one else used the bathroom so I need not fear V.D. infection, although my guide added hurriedly that all our residents had had a medical check-up.

My committee consisted of a German, a Frenchwoman, a Belgian, a Copt and a Muslim (one man, one woman) with a charming English judge as the chairman. Because French was still the universal official language, my Minutes were written in French.

33

French was also the official language in the "Mixed Courts," so judges had to be fluent even if their accents remained British. Soon after my arrival I missed a committee meeting as I was on a visit to the Bureau's Port Said office. On my return I was told that one of the committee members had demurred at my youthfulness. (Hadn't the London office realised the nature of the work she would be doing in Egypt?) To which the chairman replied in his best English accents, "Miss McCall a eu beaucoup d'experience dans la vie de prostitution, pas comme vous et moi, mais en professionelle." I was told the story again and again.

Throughout my stay in Cairo I was indebted to the Egyptian police and their English officers for all the knowledge I gained of social conditions and even for my own personal comfort. It was a police officer who found my flat for me, and he also found a servant. It was the police who obtained permission for me to observe the medical "inspection" of licensed prostitutes. This was how I described the situation in a report at the time:

As in other countries where the regulation system is still maintained, the licensed woman is generally the older or less successful woman who enters the segregated quarter to save herself the anxiety of keeping up her private clientele.Sometimes a souteneur forces his women to register so as to keep a closer watch over them, or if he is the owner of a licensed house, to fill up a gap, or provide a new attraction. Many of the women are sent from one town to another, never staying in one house more than two or three months, and finally being shipped off to Bombay or Buenos Aires.

The inspection was held every week in an unfurnished upper storey of a government building. Every registered

34

prostitute had to attend every week in order to be certified free of V.D. and get her employment card stamped. If she was on the streets without a fully stamped card she could be prosecuted or deported. It was interesting – and tragic – how many of the general public, English included, thought that licensed prostitution was a safeguard against the spread of venereal disease. They had not seen the inspection!

As I climbed the stairs to the inspection room I noticed small discarded wads of stained cotton wool. To avoid the detection of disease, the women did their own rough clean-up before the inspection, and all the officials knew this was common practise. In the middle of the bleak, rather dark inspection room stood an adjustable chair, like a dentist's chair, in which sat the woman to be examined. The doctor sat on a low chair beside her. There were no screens, no privacy. The women queued, pulled down their pants and in turn slipped into the chair as soon as it was vacated, upon which the doctor did a vaginal examination which took seconds. (At the government inspection I attended, 152 European women were dealt with in fifty minutes.) The woman then pulled up her pants, was given a stamped card and left. Anyone who did not pass was carted off to the V.D. hospital forthwith if their infection was found to be sufficiently severe, or told to report at Outpatients if the infection was mild, and not to practise their profession meanwhile. Of course they did. How else would they live? The whole process was humiliating and totally useless.

Some prostitutes boasted they could earn 10 to 15 Egyptian pounds a day at 20 piastres a time – that is 4 English shillings. They worked seven days a week, and twelve hours a day. Some had haemorrhage most of the month.

During my comfortable and secure London childhood I had been told many stories of "white slave" traffic; in my

35

mind they ranked halfway between wicked fairy stories and tales of Sherlock Holmes. But in Cairo in the late twenties, such slave traffic was a fact. In our shelter we had Armenian girls of fifteen who had been told they were coming to join a dance troupe and then found themselves forced to work in a brothel. They came to us only when they were picked up by the police. We had a young French girl who had been promised a job by a man who turned out to be a well-known Marseilles pimp. She had travelled across the Mediterranean in one of the notorious Messagerie Maritime passenger ships, concealed in a stoker's cabin. Another girl had been brought aboard in a barrel. Some of them may not have lived blameless lives in Marseilles, but few realised they would be locked up in brothels when they reached Egypt. Even if they could have escaped from the locked brothels, without passports they were fearful of asking police protection.

One French girl, under eighteen, told me her story: She came from Nîmes where she had become friendly with a man in the restaurant they both patronised. He asked her to marry him and to go to Marseilles where he lived, and he said he would find a job for her until they could fix the wedding. She married him, apparently with the consent of the two old aunts who had brought her up and with whom she lived. At Marseilles she realised that the job was prostitution on the streets, and she objected. He then introduced her to two sailors and after drinking together the three of them boarded a French ship due to sail for Alexandria. On board, she was hidden in what she described as a large pipe, where for two days she was given no food or drink. Arrived in Egypt, she was handed over to a prostitute for instruction. Her protests resulted in a sound beating. When she threatened she would go to the police they pointed out that her passport was false. They then taught her "entolage," a well-known method of stealing from customers. When the customer undressed he was asked to put his clothes on a chair in front of a curtain. Behind the curtain was a concealed opening and an accomplice removed some of the customer's cash and put it under the chair. If, when the customer put his clothes on again, he noticed the loss, the prostitute would "find" the notes and give them back to him. Girls were told not to bargain with their customers because the fee could be easily supplemented. Many men did not count their change until it was too late. Arrested and brought before the courts, this girl was sentenced to a year's imprisonment. On discharge she came to our refuge, pending deportation.

From 1927-1932 when I was in Cairo, it was said that 90% of all young male Egyptians suffered from V.D. In Cairo there were 697 licensed prostitutes (population 1,064,567) and in Alexandria with a lower population (573,063) 808 licensed prostitutes. In both cities unlicensed prostitutes probably exceeded this number.

Our shelter was useful in that it provided a half-way house for girls awaiting shipment back to their country of origin. It did nothing to discourage the trade. As long as the regulation of prostitutes (i.e. registration) continued there was very little any volunteer organisation could do about it. There were no jobs, or nearly no jobs for women in Cairo. The only success story I remember was securing the appointment of an elderly French woman as linen maid at the British hospital. Brought up in a convent, she was an excellent needlewoman. She was tired of living in a brothel, and at her own request (through the police), she had come to our shelter. The sewing room at the hospital was a haven to her. No English girls, licensed or not, were allowed to practise prostitution in Cairo and if caught they were sent back to England at once; other Consulates did little to deter their nationals from practising prostitution.

Our London office asked me to write a report on

37

conditions in Egypt, which I did, and the League of Nations published it among their papers. I doubt if it made any difference at all. But it got me an American Commonwealth Scholarship at the London School of Economics some three years later.

Among the many people I met in Cairo was Belinda Bellingham, an English journalist who had a part-time job on the Cairo weekly magazine, The Sphinx. She and I went on a holiday together, visiting Athens and then going by boat up the Dardenelles to Istanbul, which was still called Constantinople. Later she told me she was thinking of returning to England and asked if I would be interested in her part-time job on The Sphinx, reporting on social functions – which she thought I could do in the evenings. I had never worked as a journalist but the idea attracted me. I conferred with my chairman, who thought the two jobs were incompatible and probably he was right. After a short time, I decided to leave the International Bureau and I was appointed to The Sphinx full-time. The staff consisted of an alcoholic editor who was in the middle of a divorce, and a very helpful assistant editor, both English. Both went out of their way to teach me my job.

Part of my responsibilities consisted of visiting the Cairo hotels and obtaining a list of recent arrivals, some of whom I interviewed. One such visitor was Charlie Chaplin. Chaplin was on holiday in Cairo with his brother. He seemed a shy, self-effacing little man, and to me, a young and inexperienced reporter, difficult to interview. I followed the two brothers through the hotel to the open courtyard at the back of Shepheard's and watched Charlie's brother taking holiday snaps of him with what appeared to be a very small camera. Chaplin politely fended off all questions about his holiday plans, and I was too new at the job to press either of the brothers for answers.

At that time Sybil Thorndike and her entire family were

visiting Cairo. They played Shaw's St. Joan, an unforgettable experience. (Some years later I met her again when we were both sheltering in a London basement during the blitz.)

Living in Cairo certainly opened my eyes to a side of life of which I had no previous knowledge. But there was a lighter side too, since the city was a tourist centre, with plenty of dancing, tennis and wonderful expeditions into the surrounding desert. On desert excursions we usually arranged for at least two cars to travel together in case one broke down. We carried a spade in the boot and every driver had his or her own special equipment in the event of breakdown including a bit of coconut matting to put under skidding wheels. One friend pinned his faith on the silver foil in cigarette packets as a sure cure for a choked carburettor.

As a reporter on The Sphinx, I met the leader of a Cairo-to-the-Cape desert expedition, who asked me to go out with him and sample his custom-made desert car. I was naturally delighted. While I was a little surprised that in spite of his many clever gadgets he carried no spade, I assumed that apparently such an experienced desert explorer didn't have to worry about taking such old-fashioned precautions. So we set off, he and I and my spaniel puppy, our evening meal packed not just in any old tin box, but in his very special food containers. The car skimmed along much faster than my old Jowett, but I watched apprehensively as he headed for the gap between two hillocks. I had been taught to be wary: tilt one side of the car up the slope, I had been told, to avoid the blown sand which piles up between the hills. Still, he must know best, I thought. He didn't and we stuck. There was no old coconut matting to push under the wheels. No spade. The wheels spun deeper and deeper into the soft sand. It began to get dark.

39

I suggested a camel. So while Peter the spaniel and I lay down and dozed by the half-buried car, my host trudged off to the nearest village and eventually came back with a camel, a villager and a rope. There was no problem pulling us out.

From Cairo it was easy to cross the Mediterranean and visit what was then Palestine. With a woman friend I spent a weekend there and in that short time visited Jerusalem, Bethlehem and Galilee and the Black Sea.

On a trip arranged by The Sphinx, I went up the Nile by boat and saw Luxor, and Abu Simbel in its original site, which is now occupied by the Aswan Dam. I also saw Tutankhamen's tomb while the mummy was still in it. We walked down a rickety ladder and circled the tomb, an arm's length from Tutankhamen himself.

# CHAPTER 5

# Journey Through Europe

In Cairo I shared my flat with an old Oxford friend, Margaret, who had been appointed Welfare Officer to the British Consulate. Margaret was a good linguist and had lived for some years with her parents in Innsbruck. Her father was a retired civil servant. She was a much more enterprising person than I was and it was she who suggested we should travel home from Cairo together when we both had leave. My secondhand Morris Cowley was a little newer than her car, so we set off in that.

We drove to Alexandria, crossed the Mediterranean and landed in Constanza in Rumania. On the boat, through an introduction given by Russell Pasha, the British head of the Cairo police, we met Princess Ileana, the daughter of Queen Marie of Rumania. She invited us to come and have tea with her mother, the Queen, and we duly drove to their summer palace, Balcic, where we were given rose petal jam with our tea. Marie and Ileana shared a huge double bedroom in the palace. Beautiful Persian rugs were scattered over the polished floor and the place was adorned with Roman pottery urns, four feet high, filled with Arum lilies. The English lady-in-waiting and various Rumanian court officials and guests lived in another building, and a third building housed the palace's domestic staff. Lining the gravel paths throughout the grounds were more Roman pottery urns, some six or eight feet high. Queen

41

Marie wandered round her garden, secateurs in hand, wearing flowing black widow's weeds and immense leather gauntlet gloves. She was very charming and welcoming and very beautiful. (She was our own Queen Victoria's grand-daughter.) I asked if I could take her photo. "Yes my dear," she replied and promptly draped herself against a Roman urn.

We stayed a few days at Constanza and were the focus of amused interest. We had Egyptian license plates and were asked why we therefore were not black. Margaret spoke French, German and Italian, but the Rumanian menus defeated her. We found ourselves ordering curiously un-balanced meals, though a kindly local resident did his best to help us in halting French.

After we left Constanza, we stayed with a Rumanian family, friends of Margaret. There were four daughters, one of them very much like Ileana. Her father was said to have been Queen Marie's devoted lover for many years. We pressed on, neither of us at all apprehensive at the prospect of miles of deserted road nor the hazards of unknown foreign towns. We had two spare wheels and we were both well used to dealing with all-too-frequent punc-tures; cleaning plugs and carburettors had become routine with our weekend picnics in the Egyptian desert. More serious breakdowns, we thought, would have to be dealt with as best we could. Robbers and rapists did not, unlike the present days, enter into our calculations.

Many Rumanian roads were being re-made during this time, so one had a choice between skidding on deep dust which turned to liquid mud if it rained, or bumping over unrolled flints. Punctures were frequent.

At one point we had to cross the Danube, at which juncture Russell Pasha had arranged an introduction to the local chief official, who met us with some of his council, gave us lunch, which consisted of a large bowl of caviar and some wine, and then conducted us to the ford where all the local traffic had been held up to enable us to travel on the ferry first. This was a bumpy experience, successfully achieved with the help of two planks, and after bumping off the other side we drove on to Bucharest, where I inadvertently drove the wrong way down a one-way street. Amidst shouts of laughter and astonishment at seeing two women in an Egyptian car, we turned round and continued our journey. We had crossed the Carpathians on a Sunday and everyone was in local dress. We passed happy singing groups of peasants and they too all waved and shouted at the strange sight of an Egyptian car and a woman at the wheel.

In Austria we stayed in a large and gloomy castle belonging to an Austrian Count, another friend of Margaret. Ever since I had known her, Margaret had had a succession of romances, not always reciprocated, but pursued with gay abandon. Later there would usually come a period when she sadly accepted defeat, until the whole sequence was repeated in a new direction with renewed fervour. This was one such episode.

During our stay, I spent most evenings with the Count's elderly mother, who spoke little French and no English, so our conversation was limited. But she was a wise and kindly old lady who loved and understood her son.

For a week Margaret pictured herself as chatelaine of this very bleak fortress castle. Then, her illusion dispelled, we passed on.

Margaret had a one-track mind in pursuing her emotional interests of the moment. She would never hesitate to break an appointment with one of her friends without a twinge of conscience if it suited her; she seemed quite unaware of the other person's feelings or inconvenience. Yet she was an enchanting travel companion, always ready to face the next challenge. Her friends got used to her breaking appointment after appointment. When one met her again, after the exasperation had died down, she was just as charming and all was forgiven, if perhaps not forgotten.

We drove through Budapest and Vienna, stopping in each for a couple of nights and so on to Oberammergau, where the first postwar passion play was about to be performed. On the outskirts of the village our back axle broke. Somehow we got the car towed to a garage and arrived in time to see the play; we arranged to pick up the car on our return from London. Back in London we were met by our families – just in time, for I had five shillings, and that was all.

A month later we went back to Oberammergau, picked up the Morris and drove down to Naples, where we took the return boat to Alexandria.

I returned to my job on *The Sphinx*.

In 1932 both Margaret and I decided to return to England.

One of my International Bureau committee members was Mrs. Swan, wife of the Archdeacon of Cairo. She urged me to train as a social worker when I got home.

Sister Margaret Claire, with whom I had kept in touch, also advised me to train and told me of a new course of study, financed by the American Commonwealth Fund, and specialising in mental health; the profession would come to be known as psychiatric social worker, but it was still in its infancy then. She also gave me the name of Sybil Clement Brown, tutor to the course, who had herself taken the course in New York and then introduced the psychiatric social work training to England.

When I went to see Miss Clement Brown I found she had read my report to the League of Nations. She said that provided I spent a year learning about conditions in England (of which I knew nothing) I might be considered

44

for a scholarship. I decide to pursue this training, so when I returned to England, I lived with my parents, drawing on my savings and £50 very generously provided by a relative, and set about learning something of current social conditions.

For six months I worked for the Charity Organisation Society in Islington. There was then no National Health Service. Unemployment was widespread. In my abysmal ignorance and unjustified self-confidence I thought I could help men get jobs through the social contacts I had. I was soon totally disillusioned. There were no such jobs.

I was given a job in Battersea Children's Care Office, visiting families of deprived school children. I had a two-seater open Baby Austin car and, leaving it outside the schools I was visiting, I found the children discovered they could gleefully push it down the road, which they did with shouts of laughter. Terrified that they would soon learn to start it, I consulted my garage and the mechanic fitted a secret switch under the dashboard which I could turn on unobserved even with a half a dozen jeering little boys leaning across me. It did not of course stop them pushing the car, but at least they couldn't start the engine.

I visited prisons – Wandsworth, Holloway, Brixton, Leeds and several boys' Borstals. I stayed in a Dr. Barnardo's Home, sleeping in a child's bed with half my legs hanging out at the end. I stayed at a Church of England convent school, where I found on my dressing table what I took to be a grey duster with a safety pin carefully laid on top. As I was leaving my room to come down for the evening meal, a kindly Sister handed me the duster, pointing out I had not put my veil on.

In Lincolnshire I stayed at a boys' Borstal and visited the dykes they were digging in the fens. As the institution's Governor and I were crossing one of them on a plank, to my horror his standard poodle pushed past me, making the

45

plank bounce terrifyingly. With a dozen pair of eyes on me I carried on.

At the end of a year I was awarded an American Commonwealth Scholarship to study psychiatric social work at the London School of Economics.

Towards the end of 1934 my father died. There was a moving memorial service in the Temple Church in London.

CHAPTER 6

# Borstal

My visits to various charitable and statutory institutions to repair my ignorance of social conditions in England had aroused my passion for the necessity of prison reform.

A friend of mine, a barrister, was also interested in prison reform. He was a rather dull, though faithful companion, but when I found he knew something about prison conditions I found his companionship much more acceptable.

One day my father, looking very serious, had asked me to come into his study. When he had closed the door he said very gravely,

"Stephen came to see me in my chambers. He has asked for your hand." Much astonished, I said, "He can't surely have put it like that?"

"He did," replied my father. And then we both burst into laughter.

I refused, of course, and after that our dinners in Soho discussing modern prison conditions tailed off.

Once I got my Mental Health Certificate in 1935, I began searching for work. I saw an advertisement for a post in the Prison Service as Deputy Governor at Holloway Prison. I applied and was interviewed, but the appointment went to Miss Mellanby, at that time Second Mistress at Roedean. She later became a Prison Governor and finally a Prison Commissioner.

47

A week after the interview I was recalled by Mr. Alexander Patterson, one of the Prison Commissioners, and told they were considering making a further appointment on a lower scale as Assistant Housemistress. I was re-interviewed. One of the members of the panel was Miss Lilian Barker, the first woman Governor, and later, the first woman Prison Commissioner.

Miss Barker was a thick-set middle-aged woman with an iron grey Eton crop, a man's shirt and tie, a hard felt hat, stout brogue shoes and a severe grey tweed coat and skirt. She wore no make-up and this, I was to find out later, was one of her obsessions.

After the second interview by the same four- or five-man panel, I was offered the appointment of Assistant House-mistress, to be attached to the Girls' Borstal at Aylesbury for six months, followed by a transfer to Holloway Prison. My salary was £196 per year, plus board and lodging, or alternatively, a lodgings allowance.

When a few days later I reported to Miss Barker at the Aylesbury Borstal to ask when she wanted me take up the new appointment, I found she had not been officially informed of my employment and she was much put out.

"I have no room for you," she shouted. Then she added, "What do you think you are going to do?"

Taken aback, as Miss Barker had been present at both selection committees, I replied, "I have been appointed Assistant Housemistress."

I never knew whether Miss Barker had had a lapse of memory such as she had on subsequent occasions about girls' names and the like, or whether she was simply exasperated at any interruption to the daily routine. In any case, after repeated grumblings her mood suddenly changed and she slapped me on the back and very hospitably arranged to provide me with a bed. The Governor's house in Aylesbury was a short distance from the Borstal.

48

She shared it with a woman friend who was also her housekeeper. They were devoted to each other, and used to go together to a women's Masonic Lodge of which they were members. The friend was a gentle middle-aged woman, self-effacing and a welcoming hostess to me. She was the complete opposite of Miss Barker, who had a voice and a laugh that could be heard from one end of the institution to the other.

They had five dogs, a West Highland, a Great Dane and three in between.

Later I got used to Miss Barker's mood swings, the furious condemnation one moment and a slap on the back the next.

After spending a few days in the Governor's house I moved into the correctional institution itself. My bedroom was on the ground floor, small but bright. It had a bed, a washstand, a small table and a large wicker armchair which creaked. The bedcover and curtains were bright butcher blue cotton and everything, but everything, was stamped with a crown – the curtains, the blue tablecloth, the cushion and the bed linen, the tea service and even the potty beneath the bed.

Aylesbury at that time was the only girls' Borstal in England and Wales. It housed 120 girls. Scattered across the country were a number of boys' Borstals, several of which I had visited. These had housemasters, an appointment half-way between Deputy Governor and Prison Officer. At Aylesbury there was a physical training instructress but no Deputy Governor. As a result, I was looked on with curiosity by the Prison Officers and no doubt with some resentment by the Chief Officer, a woman who had spent her life in the service. In spite of my being an innovation, I found most of the officers helpful and generous in their attitude towards me.

My duties were to be in charge of the library, and to give

evening classes from five-thirty until eight, five days a week. Aside from occasional lectures by outside speakers, the institution had no other form of education, unless the embroidery, taught by the Governor, and cookery and physical training, were to be considered as "education."

Soon after my arrival I asked Miss Barker if I could see the girls' case papers. Her reply was that no one saw case histories, and that she herself never read them because "everyone must be treated alike." I found it hard to believe she had not read the case histories and totally bewildering that I, as a trained social worker, was expected to work with and live alongside these girls knowing nothing about them except what they chose to tell me. According to Miss Barker, I was not supposed to know their family background, their performance on intelligence tests, nor even the record of their previous convictions, if any. Of course, the girls I saw most of, like my library girl and the girl who cleaned my room, told me about their families, or told me what they wanted me to believe. But I was working in the dark, unnecessarily, and I could have been of much more use to them if I had known their backgrounds.

Despite her insistence on cloaking the records, Miss Barker was very highly thought of in official circles. She was a good public speaker and she had introduced some new routines in Aylesbury. One consisted of a system of promotion for the girls through five grades, beginning with Ordinary and ending with Star. Their grades were identified by different coloured collars on their uniform; white collars were worn by the highest grade, those who were hoping for their discharge, which might be advanced if their good behaviour merited it. All girls had to be discharged at the end of their standard three-year sentence. Some went out "on licence" a few months earlier.

The girls wore cotton frocks and aprons. In winter they were required to wear woolly vests and pants and, most hated of all, woollen ("lindsey") petticoats. These were bulky and shapeless. Girls went to every subterfuge to avoid wearing something which they detested. Some would pretend to have lost their petticoat. One girl, who secretly sewed neat tucks on her petticoat in an effort to make it more shapely, was made to unpick them, and then was brought before the Governor and downgraded for the offence.

During a weekly inspection, girls were lined up and an officer walked along each row, turning up their cotton frocks at the hem to see if the hated petticoat was in place. One day the inspecting officer unbuttoned each girl's frock at the neck, and to her surprise, found nothing underneath but the woolly vest. The girls had sewn a neat frill of hated flannel petticoat on to each leg of their knickers. Of course this was most reprehensible. Each girl had a "report." I couldn't help admiring their ingenuity.

Miss Barker, in many ways a bluff, generous woman, was deeply concerned for the future of her charges, and yet she had a sadistic trait which dominated her administration and produced a highly unstable atmosphere. The Governor had two obsessions. The first was make-up, which was forbidden to the girls, who would go to highly inventive lengths to find substitutes for it. Some would deliberately choose a library book with a red binding so that they could lick it. Some would steal chalk from the blackboard or flour from the kitchen or boracic powder. If their efforts were detected by the Governor, she flew into a rage so intense that it left onlookers amazed and the girls trembling.

My diary of March 9th 1935 describes an interview between my library girl and the Governor, at which I was present. The Governor accused Tommy, as the girl was usually called, of coming to see her the day before "with your face all covered with boracic powder."

51

"Do you know," the Governor continued, "that it is enough to give you spots? Have you ever known me to scrub a girl's face? Have you?"

No," replied Tommy in a low voice.

"Well I have," continued the Governor, "and when I do I take a *new* scrubbing brush and a pail of water and ordinary yellow soap and I scrub it hard and in front of all the Grades. You wouldn't like that? Well, that's what I shall do!"

This was no idle threat, I well knew.

Some years later after Miss Barker was succeeded by Miss Mellanby, the institution got a canteen and all the girls had pocket money which could be spent there. This canteen provided a number of goods including soap and make-up. A change indeed!

By regulation the Governor had to visit every day any prisoner on punishment. I remember accompanying Miss Barker on her official rounds one day shortly after I had been appointed. We visited the punishment block, where half a dozen girls, each in a separate open-ended cell, stood crushing bones to make bone meal for the garden. Each girl held a heavy stone pestle, and stroke by stroke, pounded the collection of large bones which lay at the bottom of the big stone mortar. As Miss Barker walked by, nodding good morning to each girl, she turned to me and said,

"You know why So-and-so comes here? Because she knows she will see *me* every day."

The girl smirked and said, "Yes, Madam." I think Miss Barker really believed what she said.

In many ways Miss Barker was very kind to me. I think she looked upon me as a new protégée, to be trained after her own fashion. Though she denied me access to any information about the girls, she arranged for me to visit two of the Approved Schools, one in Staffordshire and one in Kenilworth, from which some of our girls had come. (If Approved School girls absconded from their first job after they left the School, and if they were still on license, they often ended up in Borstal, even if they had been committed to the Approved School not for a crime, but "for care and protection.")

One of my more traumatic duties at Aylesbury was to attend "Board Meeting." This was a meeting chaired by the Governor and attended by the Chief Officer, her Deputy, myself and sometimes one or two other officers. Girls due for promotion to the next grade and girls hoping for their discharge would attend and state their case in faltering tones. It was a fearsome occasion which the girls dreaded for weeks beforehand. Officers' reports would be considered, but the Governor had the final decision, and the Governor tolerated nothing she interpreted as a challenge to her authority. Sometimes she mistook one girl for another. No one dared to correct her. Even the girl called by another's name did not dare to point out the mistake.

Terrible disappointment was frequent. When a girl, having reached the top grade and hoping for an early release, was told she would have to wait till the next Board because of some negative report, she left the room devastated. With no words of encouragement or sympathy, as often as not she "smashed" that night.

"Smashing" was a regular occurrence. A girl who could bear restrictions no longer would smash everything breakable in her room and tear her clothes, her sheets and often her own flesh Her screams and the banging would bring staff rushing from all sides and usually she would be put either in the padded cell or in a single punishment cell. Only too often her screams were still audible to most of the institution. Sometimes a copy-cat reaction from another girl would follow, with the same sequence. It was a highly charged emotional atmosphere few could endure passively.

Often the girl herself would take several days to return to her normal self.

Miss Barker's second obsession, and more destructive than her obsession with make-up, was her attitude towards emotional links between inmates. Being "girls" with someone meant in common parlance that A was the favourite friend of B for the time being. Attachments, as among any school girls or adolescents, swung violently from one girl to another. To the Governor and to most of the senior staff, it was always a matter for ridicule. Far from home and friends, girls were often very lonely. But to them to have a "girl" was almost essential to self-respect. Frequent switches, though sometimes traumatic, were accepted as part of life.

Most of the officers were kindly women who had left school at fourteen and worked at unskilled jobs in shops or factories. Many had had fathers in the prison service. They had to pass a fitness test, very necessary because of the long hours they had to endure on their feet; there were no chairs for officers on the exercise yards, nor sometimes in the workrooms.

One middle-aged officer was in charge of the girls who did housework in the officers' quarters. She warned me one day, in the kindest possible way, against leaving my books and personal possessions in my bedroom.

"I can't always be in your room when the girl cleans it," she said, "and I see you left out an encyclopaedia. The girl might read it."

I said I didn't mind, provided she didn't lick her finger when she turned the pages.

"Then there's your photo," she said. I had a framed photo of a portrait of my father on the table.

"I wouldn't want a girl to handle any of *my* things," she said with a shudder. "And the girl might take it into her room."

54

I thanked her and said I didn't think she would want a photo of an old man. But the officer went away shaking her head.

"You can't trust them," she said.

When I took over the library I found that most books had been rebound in black canvas and had no names on the covers. Choosing a book was therefore a lengthy procedure. So I arranged for the library girl, who was very nimble-fingered, to paint the titles and authors' names on the backs of the books. She volunteered to do this in the afternoon when the library was closed and I was off duty, but as she would be alone in the library, prison practise demanded that she be locked in until one of the officers would unlock her two hours later.

As I had no previous programme of classes to follow when I took up my appointment, I asked each class in turn what subject they would like to discuss. As they did no homework, for they were allowed no paper and had very little opportunity in our limited library to follow up any subject that interested them, the classes had to take the form of discussions. I offered them a short list of subjects which included foreign countries, current events, biographies, social insurance, pensions and unemployment benefits. Their favourite subject was current events (or "coloured events" as one girl innocently called it); out of my first hundred classes, forty-one were on this subject. The next favourite subject was foreign countries. They wanted to know how people from similar backgrounds to their own lived elsewhere. What were their homes like? Their wages? What did they eat? As their knowledge of geography was usually nil, I used to put a large map on the board and show what countries you travelled through, what seas you crossed to reach the country we were discussing. Most of the girls had little or no idea what subject they wanted to discuss – any subject was preferable

55

to being locked up in your room, and so attendance was 100%.

I wrote to my sister Nita that what I needed was a good reference library. As always she rose to the occasion and sent me, in twelve volumes, Everyman's Encyclopaedia. It was invaluable. It still is.

I tried to institute debates, but they proved too difficult for the girls were too shy and too inarticulate to attempt them. So sometimes we played a game where members of the two sides asked each other questions on the lecture I had just given, and scored points if they got the right answer. It was most helpful to me as I learnt what had been absorbed and what had gone over their heads.

Invariably I found the junior grades the most responsive; the senior girls could think of nothing but how soon they would be out. They were disillusioned and cynical. The younger girls had some hope, and were anxious to make a good impression, but the older ones had often given up hope.

In one class I had a totally silent junior girl on whom I seemed to make no impression. Then, by chance, the subject of spinning was mentioned in class one day and at once she brightened. She knew about that, she said. She had worked in a spinning factory in Lancashire. If only I had seen her case papers and had known that, I could have saved a lot of wasted time and wasted effort! After this day she became one of the most attentive girls in the class.

I taught every girl throughout the institution. Some came to two classes a week, and a few, to three. One day I passed two girls scrubbing the long corridor side by side, heads together. They were quizzing each other about last night's class. It made all the preparation seem worthwhile.

As I would note later:

Aylesbury was full of cases which would have benefited

from psychotherapy. Day after day, I saw the same types I had met and worked with as a psychiatric social worker in child guidance clinics and in mental hospitals. But there was no psychiatrist [at the institution] qualified to treat them, and there was no question of their being sent to a clinic outside the institution.

# CHAPTER 7

# Holloway

I left Aylesbury with mixed feelings. I was genuinely sorry to say goodbye to the 120 girls whose names I had so laboriously learnt. I had never been good at remembering names, and I used to keep a chart on my desk at every class showing where the girls sat, and as they called out their names I would try to scribble some identifying mark – curly hair, blue eyes, whatever. Their uniforms were of course identical except for the grade collars. I also tried hard to learn some details about the background of each girl – her hometown, her family past, her last job. It would all have been so much easier if I could have been given access to their case histories.

Of course I had visited them all at one time or another in their rooms, sometimes about library books, sometimes just in an effort to make contact. But the Chief Officer looked on visits with the gravest suspicion. I must be sure to keep the door open, she warned. You never knew!

Moving to Holloway prison in 1936, again as assistant housemistress, was a welcome relief after Aylesbury's overcharged emotional atmosphere. None of the sinister implications were attributed to relationships between women prisoners there; the staff was generally good-tempered, level-headed and concerned for the welfare of their charges.

Holloway was administered by a Governor, Dr. Morton,

a male medical doctor. (No women's prison at the time had a female governor, except Aylesbury.) He was a thoughtful, caring person, and I was often invited to his house to meet his family. Sadly he fell ill, and shortly before I left, he died. He was greatly missed.

The Deputy Governor, Mary Size, was a charming woman who later was promoted to Governor in one of the newer women's prisons. When I arrived at Holloway she invited me to share her flat until I found accommodation of my own. I decided I had had enough of furnished officer's quarters and their crown-embellished equipment, so I found a flat within a short distance of the prison.

For my first month Miss Size arranged very sensibly that I should accompany some of the officers in their daily duties, beginning with unlocking the cells first thing in the morning. None of the cells had toilets in those days and my most vivid memory of that first month is the smell that hit you as you unlocked each cell. Though there were bells in each cell, the inmates – in those days only one to each cell – usually preferred not to subject themselves to the long wait often involved in answering it and used the pail provided. In the morning women lined up to wash and to empty their pails and sluice them out in one of the all too few lavatories – four lavatories to fifty cells. The stench was appalling. Some women had been shut up for thirteen hours. Some were menstruating. Some had diarrhoea. If they had been admitted the night before they might have come in drunk and vomited all over the floor. Today, "slopping out" is incredibly still part of prison life in most prisons. And there is now more than one prisoner to each cell.

I was given a set of keys on a long and wide leather belt. After making necessary new holes in it to keep it from slipping off, I devised a scheme for putting an elastic band round the keys so that they did not jangle with my every step. It was a noise which I found intolerable and which I felt the prisoners must dislike just as much. My elastic band caused some laughter, but also drew approving smiles from the prisoners.

Miss Size had no prejudice, like Miss Barker, about ignorance of women's backgrounds somehow guaranteeing fairer treatment and I was allowed to see any case papers I requested. Unlike Aylesbury, however, prisoners came and went all too frequently and of course there were many more than the 120 Borstal girls. With such a constant turnover, it was particularly difficult to learn names.

After a month of doing ordinary prison officer's duties, I was allocated to my own duties. Most of my work, Miss Size told me, would be with the young prisoners. I could arrange classes for them, as I had at Aylesbury. Attendance was compulsory, but as at Aylesbury, any diversion from being locked up was welcome. Because of their greater diversity and often greater sophistication, I found it more difficult to hold the attention of my student prisoners at Holloway. But because I was younger than most of the officers and very obviously new, they were kind and courteous.

It was also my responsibility to visit classes being given by outside teachers. One such was an embroidery class (prison authorities had a strange idea that embroidering tray cloths was a suitable occupation for brothel keepers and petty thieves) and the teacher was new and nervous. As I came into one of her first classes, she hastened to make way for me in the small, crowded classroom and inadvertently pushed the door closed as I entered. I heard a fatal click; prison classroom doors have no keyhole and no handle on the inside, so my master key was useless. The women were delighted and hooted with laughter.

"That's all right," I said with as much dignity as I could muster, "I'll ring the bell."

*Sir Robert McCall, K.C.V.O., K.C. (my father) – Cartoon by "Spy"
for "Vanity Fair"*

*Geoffrey McCall and his mother, ?1900*

*Lady McCall (my mother), ?1904*

*Cicely McCall, 1905*

*Sieleç, 1923*

*Princess Tildy Czartoryska and her children, 1923*

*Shooting Party at Baskow, Princess Tildy Czartoryska on the extreme left with Cicely next to her, 1924*

*Queen Marie and Ileana, 1930*

*A Cairo registered prostitute (French), 1930*

*On the way home from Cairo in the Morris Cowley, 1930*

*Devon and Exeter Approved School garden girls, 1936*

*Rosamund Dashwood, Cicely, Lionel Dashwood – Croyle, Devon, 1937*

*Cicely, Elizabeth Dashwood (E. M. Delafield), Paul Dashwood and Rosamund*

*Cicely, 1938*

*The End House, 1959*

*The End House and author, 1968*

*Cicely, 1978*

*Cicely, 1990*

*The End House, 1993*

Their laughter redoubled.

"You can ring, Miss," they said between their gasps, "But no one will come." And for some minutes no one did come. At last, realizing that no prisoner would have the effrontery to ring as repeatedly as I was ringing, an alarmed officer ran down the corridor and unlocked us.

After that day I learnt to shoot the lock when I was on the wrong side of the door.

When I told Miss Size of my adventure, she laughed. There was none of the emotional uproar there would have been at Aylesbury, had I dared to tell the Governor.

Miss Size was anxious that, as a newcomer, I should learn all sides of prison service. So when Mrs. Rattenbury, a prisoner who had been accused of murdering her husband, went on trial, she arranged that I should accompany her to the Old Bailey, together with two attendant prison officers. The officers wore uniforms; I did not, and was described by the press as the prison doctor! I sat with her in the dock every day throughout her trial.

During these many weeks, Mrs. Rattenbury was kept in Holloway's prison hospital, where I sometimes visited her. She was an overweight woman, not easy to make contact with. When she exercised in the prison yard with the other prisoners awaiting trial, she wore her own clothes, including a fur coat, which made her easily recognisable from a distance. Convicted prisoners, if they got the chance, would peer out of the corridor windows and whisper, "That's 'er." Most of them thought her guilty and predicted that she would be hanged. If so, she would be the first woman to be hanged in Holloway for many years.

The officials, too, were proceeding on the assumption that the prisoner would be convicted and hanged. As so many years had passed since the last hanging, the condemned cell block was being redecorated. A new W.C. was to be installed for use in the three weeks the condemned prisoner would spend in it between the passing of the sentence and her death. Plumbing had to be attended to. There also had to be sufficient room for the two prison officers who would always be in attendance in relays throughout the twenty-four hours.

I asked Miss Size how they would spend their time. She said they would play "Ludo" and cards. Even when the prisoner went to the lavatory she would have to be accompanied. Not for one moment must she be out of their sight.

There was also, of course, the execution room to be brought up to date.

All these quarters were situated on the first floor in the middle of the prison. Workmen passed up and down the passage carrying ladders and equipment. The hammering was continuous.

One day as I was standing talking to one of the officers, one of the prisoners rushed up to us.

"I can't stand it," she cried. "Please, please may I be moved to another wing? Anywhere away from this noise!"

The officer was sympathetic, and alternative arrangements were made.

As the weeks of the trial passed, the atmosphere on that landing was unbearably tense.

I wished that some of the people in favour of capital punishment could experience the horror it generated among the women occupying adjacent cells. The officers too were tense. They knew that if Mrs. Rattenbury was convicted they would have to share the duties of guarding her for those three weeks of waiting. Two of them would have to lead her – or carry her – to the scaffold. I was told that after the last hanging in Holloway, one of the officials present committed suicide, and two others left the service. Certainly when I was there there was a deep dread among the rank and file prison officers that they would be called upon to participate.

On the last day of the trial, two officers and I accompanied Mrs. Rattenbury as usual to the Old Bailey. While the judge was considering his verdict we waited below the dock. One of the court officials, presumably medical, came up to me and asked if I would enquire from Mrs. Rattenbury when she had her last menstrual period. If there was any chance of her being pregnant she could not be hanged. Mrs. Rattenbury was surprised when I asked her this, but was too bemused to draw conclusions, too wrapped up in her own thoughts.

The verdict was acquittal. Mrs. Rattenbury's chauffeur/lover was convicted of the murder. Once the verdict was read, we hurried her out of the dock, down the stairs and away by a side door where there was a waiting taxi. Inside it was her kind sister-in-law, who had been in court every day. As we bundled Mrs. Rattenbury through the side door, she turned to me and said "Thank you," and pushed a bar of chocolate into my hand.

A few weeks after returning home, she walked into the sea and drowned herself.

It was some weeks after the trial, when I was getting breakfast in my flat, when I heard a ring at the door. It was Tommy, my former library girl at the Aylesbury borstal.

Before I left Aylesbury there had been various incidents which had helped to disturb Tommy's precarious emotional balance. First she had been promised her discharge but then it had been deferred for a minor infringement of the rules. Then she had been given a provisional date which had not been honoured. Tommy had asked to go to London on her discharge but instead the Governor had offered her a position in a Luton laundry at 17/6d. per week.(The Governor had told me that the laundry had promised in exchange to make a donation to the Aylesbury

63

After Care Fund, and that this Fund would subsidise Tommy if need be.) When I left Aylesbury I was told that no one in the prison service was allowed to correspond with a prisoner. So it was only some months later that I first heard from Tommy. She wrote me at Holloway and said she had been discharged on licence and was living somewhere in the Midlands. I replied and sent her my best wishes for her new freedom. I described my new flat and told her proudly about my freshly planted window boxes.

As she sat in my flat that morning Tommy told me about her life. She had found the laundry very hard work and the speed of the work required was more than she could manage. At first she had been given chefs' caps to iron and had done these satisfactorily because she had ironed nurses' and cooks' caps at Aylesbury. Then she was switched to men's shirts, but the collars and cuffs took longer than the time she was allowed and she was warned that unless she worked faster her pay would be reduced. Lonely and unhappy with no friend or family to turn to and fearful of dismissal, she walked out one day. She had thumbed a lift, walked some of the way, slept "rough," and finally arrived on my doorstep.

I told her I would have to report her arrival to the prison authorities. She was not surprised. She seemed resigned, grateful not to be turned away immediately.

I suggested she should have a bath and wash her underclothes and told her I would return later. I also told her to help herself to whatever leftovers there were in the kitchen.

Then I went at once to report to Miss Size. She was clearly worried. Everything that had happened was most unusual and definitely against Standing Orders, she said. Prisoners on licence didn't turn to prison officers for help. Dear Miss Size! She was concerned for Tommy, but most of all she was deeply concerned at what Miss Barker, newly appointed Prison Commissioner, would say to me. Miss Barker was due to visit Holloway that very morning.

Miss Barker was astounded and furious. When I said I had left Tommy in my flat having a bath, her astonishment and fury knew no bounds. How could I let Tommy use my bathroom, she asked. Didn't I know she might be infected? It was the old, old assumption that every lawbreaker was potentially infected and that V.D. could be passed on almost with the touch of a hand. Tommy, she shouted, must of course be returned to Aylesbury at once and must serve out the rest of her prison sentence. She would be housed with the other licence-revoked girls, who occupied a special wing and had no privileges.

A week later, when Tommy's belongings had been searched, my letter to her was discovered and I had a further interview with Miss Barker. I had written in most unsuitable terms, said Miss Barker. Searching my memory for what I had said, I remembered the window boxes. Of course, not official language at all! Did I realise, Miss Barker went on, that this would jeopardise my promotion?

If I had not left the service, perhaps it would indeed have done so – at least for as long as Miss Barker remained a Commissioner.

As all correspondence was banned, I heard nothing more of Tommy for a year. Then she wrote to say she was now free. She had served her full term. She continued to write to me from time to time. She married. In the war she got a job in a cinema and became one of the first women to be employed as a projectionist. One day, when I was driving through the town where she lived, I had an evening meal with her. Tommy introduced me to her husband. She had told him I was someone she had met when she was at school – an old friend. And so I felt I was. She gave me ham and stewed apricots and generous slices of bread and butter. She had four small daughters and the youngest was called Cicely.

Tommy had been a foster child. She had never known her mother, who had been unmarried. She told me that her foster brother, who she believed was her blood brother, knew who her mother was but refused to tell her.

Highly intelligent and very determined, Tommy had always attracted other girls and so was constantly in Miss Barker's bad books. Yet she bitterly resented the implications of homosexuality and said to me once that when she got out she wanted to have nothing more to do with the girls. It was typical of the Borstal atmosphere that the implication of lesbianism was constantly being thrown at her. Many other girls must have felt the same way.

I have only once been back to Holloway since I left the prison service. I went to visit a woman accused of murder and later acquitted. She lived in West Suffolk where I was at that time a parliamentary candidate. The woman was, as is usual for women accused of murder, housed in the prison's hospital wing. I brought her some flowers but was not allowed to hand them to her; they had to be taken away and searched for drugs or lethal instruments. The prison officer remained in the room with me during our visit, and though there was only one chair in the room, I was sternly reproved when I perched myself on the side of the bed. So I sat on the hard wooden chair and the prisoner and the officer stood. It was not a very helpful visit.

After leaving Holloway, I wrote "They Always Come Back," a book based on my experience there and at Aylesbury. It was published by Methuen in 1938, with a foreword by my friend the writer E.M. Delafield, about whom more later. The book was anecdotal in style and my intention was that it be influential in promoting prison reform. It ended:

Institutions must always be artificial. At best they provide an interval – a convalescence – in which a girl can have time and opportunity to think, and time to outgrow some of her undesirable habits. Institutional treatment indefinitely prolonged – stretched over late childhood and early womanhood – defeats its own ends. It is no longer an interval, interposed to check certain tendencies or to encourage others, it is a slice of life – in some cases the whole of girlhood. It is no longer preparing a girl to be a useful citizen. It is substituting another and an artificial life for her own free life. However shiftless or even anti-social her life may have been, there are ways of helping to adjust a misfit other than shutting her away from the difficulties which she has been unable to face. "They always come back," say the officers.

But need they?

Today these convictions may seem innocent in a society as troubled by social problems as ours has been. But they still affirm my belief that people behave with the same kind of consideration as that with which they are treated. I would have the opportunity to witness this again in my next position.

CHAPTER 8

# Exeter Approved School

One day at Holloway Prison, when I had been assistant housemistress for over a year, I had a call from the Home Office asking me to go and see one of the principal secretaries in charge of Home Office schools. On arrival I was told that there had been a crisis at the Devon and Exeter Senior Approved School for Girls: the recently appointed headmistress had been picked up by the police in the street in Exeter, drunk and incapable. The approved school's staff was in a state of shock. Could I go down there temporarily and take charge? And if I felt like considering it, would I perhaps stay on as headmistress? I said I would certainly go temporarily and would consider the second proposal later. My interviewer relaxed and asked if I could go the next day.

My salary would be just under £200 a year plus board and lodging, I was told. (My salary in the prison service had been £192 plus lodgings allowance.)

Making my explanations to Holloway, the next day I locked up my flat and drove down to Devon in my old Baby Austin.

The school was a long two-storey building on the outskirts of Exeter. On the ground floor there were two classrooms, kitchen, dining room, and the headmistress's office and sitting room. The first floor had three staff bedrooms, several single girls' rooms, and the headmistress's bedroom. This bedroom had a second door opening on to the large dormitory with a spy-hole in the bedroom door. The dormitory had thirty beds. There was no heating on the first floor.

On my arrival the staff told me they had made up a bed for me in one of the girls' single rooms because they had not yet been able to get rid of the smell of alcohol that permeated the headmistress's bedroom. The built-in cupboard there had been scrubbed several times after the removal of the empty bottles, but still the smell remained.

My predecessor had, I think, been in office only a matter of weeks, but I was never clear about just when the staff first suspected that her habits were not strictly sober, nor when the matter came to the attention of the School Committee. Perhaps the staff felt it was not proper for them to report on the behaviour of their senior. But it is hard to believe they didn't notice it.

The staff consisted of an elderly assistant headmistress, a nice old body who would have been a pleasant housekeeper for an elderly employer, but was quite out of touch with modern life or the younger generation. Her salary was £80 a year, and when she retired – which she soon did – the Committee agreed to offer £100 a year to her successor. This enabled me to appoint a pleasant middle-aged woman with experience working in Church of England hostels. There was also a cook and a sewing instructress, and a schoolteacher who left shortly after my appointment and who I replaced with a charming young Girl Guide captain, energetic and wholly admirable. The school also employed a very old gardener. He provided the school with vegetables, and he had a large greenhouse in which he grew chrysanthemums and tomatoes.

Before the appointment of the alcoholic headmistress the school had been under the charge of a former village schoolmistress who had become pensionable. She was of the old-school type and beat the girls; the gardener told me how he used to be called in to hold them down while she beat the palms of their hands with a ruler or a cane. Yet many of them loved her. After my appointment some asked me if they could visit her in her retirement, and of course I agreed. Others, however, hated and feared her.

I found a little book of rules tucked away in a cupboard, which gave the punishments that the school had meted out to transgressors in the early years of the twentieth century. At that time children of eleven were admitted. For being "rude to matron" the statutory punishment was having their hair cut off.

In the garden at the bottom of four or five stone steps, I found a brick shed some five feet by three feet with a domed ceiling and stone floor. I had to stoop to enter. The gardener kept his tools there. It had a stout wooden door with an iron bar and padlock. Curious about its origin, I asked the gardener. "It's where they used to shut the naughty girls for punishment," he replied.

The girls' daily routine was to spend a certain number of hours in the sewing room, a certain number in the school-room, and for some, a certain number in the kitchen or garden. A member of the staff herded them from one room to another. When they spoke to me they added, "Please Mum" to any reply they made. Thus, when I entered the classroom, there was a chorus of "Good morning please'um"s. I told them my name was Miss McCall, not "Please 'm," but it took weeks to break them of the habit. They would even say "Goodnight please 'm." At long last my ill-suppressed giggles persuaded them that they could use my name without any addition.

Perhaps the most rewarding result of my work was to see frightened, half-starved little girls developing after a few months into young people who were healthier, more normal and smiling. In spite of their appalling backgrounds

70

(only two out of fifty girls had both mother and father living at home) they all, or very nearly all, wanted to return home. The promise of home leave was the greatest incentive for good behaviour I could hold out. The duration of their stay varied, but the maximum was two years and for most it was much less. When they left they were on license, under the supervision of their local probation officer. Legally they could be recalled, but they seldom were.

There were between thirty and forty girls at the school when I arrived and the numbers soon rose. They came from all over England and Wales and ranged in age from sixteen to seventeen and a half. Their parents ranged from a clergyman's widow in Hereford to a Tilbury dock worker. The clergyman's widow's only regret at her daughter's placement was that she would now be "among working-class girls." Most of the other parents were thankful their daughters were at last, they hoped, getting some training.

To my surprise, I found on arriving that the thirty girls who slept in the big dormitory undressed in darkness because there were no electric light bulbs in the sockets. I suggested this should be remedied. What I didn't realise was that the dormitory windows had no adequate curtains, and the first night the light bulbs were in place there was pandemonium in the street outside when our adolescent girls started to undress in full view of passers-by. Not one of my staff thought to warn me about the lack of curtains; I suppose they had been so accustomed to obey the old headmistress that no order she gave was ever questioned. The same obtuseness made our housekeeper unaware of the cause of the foul smell that pervaded the corridor until I drew her attention to the fire buckets, which had been used as urinals by the girls at night. No staff had noticed, it seemed.

When I arrived the girls wore school gym tunics and

71

blouses on Sundays, and shapeless cotton frocks and long white aprons during the week. Gradually I persuaded the School Committee to let me buy some more normal clothing for our adolescents, and great was the excitement when we acquired dungarees for the garden girls.

School meals were strictly segregated. The girls ate first and later the staff, using separate cutlery and china. My meals were served in my sitting room. I suggested to the staff that we should all eat together and have the same food. They were horrified.

"We couldn't use the same cutlery and plates," they said. I pointed out that these were washed, and added that our school was the only one in England that did not accept any girl who had V.D. Nevertheless, their fear was unallayed.

"We don't know what we might catch," they pleaded.

I persisted, and finally we all had our first communal midday meal together. I was the only person in the room who ate. Plates were sent away untouched. Girls and staff alike were horrified at eating in each other's presence. The next day, hunger won. I used to move to a different table every day and the girls were free to sit where they liked. But I never persuaded the staff to eat at the girls' tables until much later, when new staff replaced the old and we all mixed freely.

In an effort to break down the artificial atmosphere of communal living, I began to invite half a dozen senior girls at a time to spend an hour in my sitting room on a Sunday evening, just sitting around the coal fire, talking and having tea and a scone. It was touchingly appreciated, and it became a regular practise. The girls would sit on the floor in my small room, beaming from ear to ear, and talk about their homes. Sometimes we made toast. When later I acquired a Cairn puppy, she was an added attraction. This seemed a very simple way to give enormous pleasure to deprived youngsters. It endorsed my conviction that no school, however hard one tries, can ever take the place of home, however bad home may have been.

One summer I took the girls to camp. We booked a barn in a farmyard in Cornwall near the coast and some forty girls under the supervision of my nice young schoolteacher and myself travelled by coach and spent a fortnight bathing in the sea and playing cricket on the village green. One intrepid village boy joined us and remained our constant companion for the whole holiday. Our food was cooked on a camp fire under the expert eye of our young teacher.

In preparation for our holiday I had had new cotton frocks made in our workroom for each girl. There were six different colors and they chose their own. I also bought bathing dresses and amidst embarrassed giggles we had a dress parade/fashion show before we left. I told them that if anyone absconded during our holiday this innovation would never be repeated. No one did.

My most vivid memory is of standing in shallow sea water holding up giggling girls and getting colder and colder. All the girls learnt to swim. I was very proud of them.

The holiday was a great success, but girls running away from the school itself was a problem I never solved. When I came to Exeter everything was locked – the front door, the classroom doors when not in use, and of course every cupboard. I unlocked the doors and the girls walked out. They were brought back by the police. Discussion, explanations, punishments – nothing seemed to make much difference. It was always the few who ran away; the majority never did. I had to lock the doors, but looking back on it I still think opening them was an experiment worth trying. Certainly the majority responded.

Working at the Exeter school was, without doubt, the most arduous task I have ever undertaken. My original

73

staff, though devoted and willing, and used to working twelve hours a day, were incapable of taking responsibility; no doubt under the old headmistress they had never been expected to. When I came back from an afternoon off I would be greeted by a list of "disasters" that had occurred in my absence. Mary had been rude to so-and-so, Jane had stolen a piece of cake, Jean had been found at the end of the garden and she shouldn't have been there and Doreen had lost her vest. "Can't she go on looking for it?" I asked. No, apparently not; this was a major disaster, it seemed. Nothing could ever be taken lightly. Nothing could be laughed at.

On my appointment to the school, one of the lecturers on the Mental Health Course I had taken at the London School of Economics, Dr. Posthuma, gave me an introduction to a friend of hers, Elizabeth Dashwood – E. M. Delafield, author of Diary of a Provincial Lady – who lived at Cullompton, not far away. She was also a J. P. and interested in the school. We became great friends. Her house and the normal family life she lived provided me with a much needed refuge from the high level of stress that so often prevailed at the school. She helped me keep a sense of humour. I owed more than I could ever repay to her and her family.

At the end of two years at the Devon and Exeter school, I was offered a job in London as editor of the magazine run by the National Council for Women.

Because I was never really off-duty at Exeter, and non-residential work sounded to me a very desirable change, I accepted. Elizabeth also suggested I should take over her share of her London flat, part of which was being occupied by her friend Lorna Lewis. Lorna was a journalist and wrote children's stories. She was Zoo correspondent for the Sunday Express, and I had got to know her in Devon. She had stayed with me at the Devon and Exeter

School – in some discomfort – and we had much in common.

It was 1938 and I was thirty-eight. Only a few weeks after I began my new job, I contracted flu. A heart attack followed. My doctor, years later, told me she had given me only another five years to live. She was wrong. I convalesced with the Dashwoods for a month and Elizabeth's children, Lionel and Rosamund, carried me up and down the stairs in a chair every day from bedroom to garden. During this process, both children were convulsed with laughter. Rosamund particularly thought it hilarious, and the chair rocked perilously but I never actually overturned.

It was a very happy, carefree month. I never had any further heart attacks and this is still true fifty years later.

# CHAPTER 9

# Educational Organizer and Psychiatric Social Worker

The high regard in which the National Federation of Women's Institutes is held today is due almost wholly to the vision and commitment of Lady Denman, its Chairman. She held the conviction that ordinary countrywomen had a great part to play in the development of rural life, and that this had not previously been realised to the full. Women's Institutes, she believed, had far more to give to village life than making jam and patchwork quilts. She wanted to open Institute members' eyes to a wider vision, to lead them to think about and work for improved social conditions in the villages, including better water supply, better schools, and improved telephone service. Her hope was that this work would ultimately equip women to play an expanded role in local and national government in the future. So, in the late 1930s, with war clouds gathering, she determined that alongside the Women's Institutes Handicraft Organiser, the Marketing Organiser and the General Organiser there should be an additional section: the Educational Organiser.

Among the people she consulted about who might lead this new project was Elizabeth Dashwood, who was a member of the N.F.W.I. Executive and a popular speaker to W.I.s and other organisations. When Elizabeth recommended me as the first Education Organiser, I was asked to lunch by Lady Denman, together with Elizabeth and half a dozen other executive committee members – a rather formidable form of interview. In spite of my being appointed at a higher rate of salary than the other organisers, I found my fellow organisers wonderfully supportive and keenly interested in this new endeavour. Vera ("Peter") Cox, the Marketing Organiser, I had met before and we had much in common. Later, at her request, I wrote the N.F.W.I. pamphlet on marketing.

There were three other organisers at the National Federation headquarters, and Betty Christmas, who was particularly concerned with the formation of the new W.I.s, soon became everybody's favourite. Betty was young, modest and desperately anxious to make good in this, her first responsible job. She had a delicious sense of humour and was always willing to fill in if an extra pair of hands was needed.

There was also the Handicraft Organiser, Miss Armes, whose skills and enthusiasm were responsible for the high standard of handicraft for which W.I.s were already famous. She organised the yearly handicraft exhibition, which was held in the Albert Hall in London, and was patronised by Queen Mary.

In Adeline Vernon, I had an enthusiastic chairman of my education sub-committee, and she and I went on many county tours together. The usual routine was to spend a week per month in the Eccleston Street Headquarters to attend committees and write reports, and three weeks touring the counties. In my eight years with the W.I.s I visited every county in England and all but one of the Welsh counties. The W.I.s provided a car, and each organiser averaged 15,000 to 20,000 miles per year.

On our travels, we were usually lodged by W.I. members, except in Durham, where so many miners were out of work that hospitality was not possible for their hard-

77

pressed wives. Our lodgings were always unpredictable, and often we didn't know when we set out on a Monday morning whether we would be staying that night in a rectory, a very simple cottage or a palatial country house. In the war years we took our rations with us. I remember one hostess, Master of the local hunt, saying apologetically during the early years of the war that since they now had an entire evacuated school living in the house I might never get my suitcase unpacked as they were down to "just the head housemaid." The change was apparent as I drove up to their stately door and saw dozens of Wellington boots of all sizes parked on both sides of the marble steps. But we still had pheasant and melon for dinner. I remember handing the butler my miserable little rations of butter, margarine and sugar.

Some time after war had been declared I felt that perhaps I should be doing more for the war effort. I telephoned Lady Denman and said I was considering joining the Services. I have never heard her more vehement. Didn't I realise I was helping to prepare women for after the war? Wasn't that more important than joining up and being relegated to some clerical job in a barracks? Very subdued, I agreed, and stayed on.

In the 1940s, conditions in many parts of rural England were still deplorable. The Women's Institutes passed a resolution in 1943 that water supply, electricity and sewerage should become a national responsibility and that local authorities should be compelled to take action to ensure as good a supply in the country as in the towns. To back up this resolution a questionnaire on available water supplies was issued to every W.I. throughout the country and replies were received from 3,500 villages. One of my responsibilities was to summarise the replies. The final report was widely distributed, was quoted in the House of Commons debate and received wide press coverage. It gave a fascinating though horrifying account of living conditions in rural England. In most villages few houses had indoor sanitation. There was no piped water, and many villagers had to carry water from a standpipe more than the 200 feet which was the current statutory distance within which a landlord should provide water. Some schools had no water supply at all, and the great majority had "earth closets" and not many of them. Almshouses were no better off. In Northamptonshire eight almshouses shared two earth closets. Here is an excerpt from the report I wrote at the time:

The lack of water [for sewerage] and the polluted water used by many country people causes endless unnecessary labour and is a real menace to health. But the description given by Institutes of the lack of sanitation is appalling.

Twenty-six counties estimate that over half the number of houses surveyed have earth, bucket or chemical closets. Some buckets are emptied by the local authority once a week or once a fortnight. Since the black-out this is generally done by day and the pails stand waiting to be emptied along the village street. In the majority of villages, pails are emptied by the householder, and contrary to the popular conception of country life, many cottages have no garden. This means that the pails have to be carried down the road to a field or a ditch or a stream where the contents can be turned out. At Maiden Newton (Dorset) 6 houses have to carry buckets 20 yards down the main road to their gardens or allotments, 131 out of 163 houses have earth or bucket lavatories. In Lindsell (Essex) the school earth closets are emptied 3 times a year. Effluent from various cesspits runs into a ditch near the school just to add to the general odour.

Thirty-five out of the 49 householders of Frome Vauchurch (Dorset) have earth or bucket closets and the majority empty them into the river. Ten houses have no garden as an alternative. At Debenham (E. Suffolk) women carry their lavatory pails a quarter of a mile in order to empty them.

The N.F.W.I. had long provided conferences to train women on committee procedures and now we added to these by organising speakers' schools. If W.I. members of the future were to play their part in local government they must not only know accepted procedure but they must also be articulate enough to negotiate it effectively.

As the war proceeded petrol was severely rationed and many cross-country journeys had to be taken by train. By this time Lorna Lewis and I had moved from Elizabeth Dashwood's primitive Doughty Street flat (which had no kitchen), first to a top-floor flat with a roof garden, almost next to King's Cross Station, and then, as bombing increased, to a ground- and first-floor flat recently vacated by Lorna's mother in Swan Court, Chelsea. In September 1941 Swan Court was hit. It was five in the afternoon when the bomb burst. I was at home and was giving shelter to Mary, our nervous fifth-floor flat neighbour.

My guest and I had been looking out of the window when a passerby called up, "He's just overhead." We retreated hastily and just then the bomb fell on the flat at the back of ours. When the dust subsided I was standing in debris at the head of the single-flight staircase; behind us, where the next-door flat had been, there was a heap of smouldering rubble and beyond it an open space.

An air raid warden appeared from nowhere, a Pekinese in his arms.

"Is this yours?" he said.

No," I replied, rather crossly.

Slowly and carefully I freed first one leg and then the other from the rubble which surrounded me, astounded to be alive. "Everything works," I told myself as I shook off the debris. But there was no sign of my sheltering guest.

I managed to get to the window, and seeing a man in the street I shouted "Help!" Then I felt embarrassed. How theatrical and absurd it sounded!

Looking out of the window I saw that the ground-floor casement windows were open. I climbed out and just managed to reach the window sill. I called to the man in the street, and he and I both went back into the flat through the ground-floor windows to look for Mary. I could see nothing but dust and rubble. Then, in the middle of the pile of debris which had been the staircase, I saw a trickle of blood. We both dug frantically, tossing aside lumps of plaster and concrete, till Mary emerged. Her head was bleeding but she could stand. A Red Cross worker appeared (without a Pekinese) and Mary was led off to the First Aid station. Apart from the cut, her only injury was a cracked collar bone. I was bruised back and front but no bones were broken. I hung around in the street outside our block, waiting for Lorna to return from her A.R.P. station, and hoping she would see me before she saw the heap of rubble which had been our home.

As I waited in Swan Lane for Lorna to arrive, a forlorn group of Swan Court residents huddled together on the pavement. One woman was naked except for a towel. She had been having a bath when the bomb fell.

When Lorna arrived we took a taxi to Markham Square where we knew my old friend Dorothy would take us in. As I sat down in the taxi my nylon stockings tore across each knee, and this seemed to me the last straw! Nylons were near-unobtainable. Here was I, alive after a direct hit, and I had ruined this much prized possession! I nearly cried.

81

During the blitz most people were naturally frightened and after this experience I was much more frightened when I had to spend a night in London. But unlike participants in the Gulf War, no one talked of their fears then. There were no "support groups" for bereaved families, and fears were shamefacedly buried. "Not another bomb story," friends would say tartly.

After I spent two days in bed at Markham Square, my sister Nita suggested that I should stay with her in her house in Tiddington, Oxfordshire. I stayed in bed there for a few more days, still very stiff and bruised, but returned to work a fortnight later. There followed three of the saddest months in my life. Within a few weeks, Christopher, Nita's eldest son, was killed in the R.A.F. Shortly after this Nita was told nothing more could be done for her cancer, and before Christmas, she died. Meanwhile my mother, aged ninety, who had been living with Nita, deteriorated and became more and more confused, and I had to take her to an old people's home. Although it had been carefully explained to her and she had agreed to go, since Nita was terminally ill, when at the end of a long day's drive we drew up at the door of the nursing home, she looked at the name board and turning to me said, "So this is what you have done to me." She walked in, erect as ever, without a backward glance. No explanation was possible. Of course later she accepted it and appreciated being near my older sister, who had been evacuated to the same Hertfordshire village. But that moment is one I shall never forget. I felt I had betrayed her.

After Nita's death I decided not to return to London, where Lorna had been taken in by Dorothy, our kind Markham Square friend. Shortly after, I bought a cottage in Oxfordshire, convenient for the evacuated N.F.W.I. Headquarters, which had moved to Oxford.

"Willows," named by Elizabeth Dashwood, was a Cotswold stone, two-bedroom cottage, alongside a little stream. When I bought it, it had been empty for many years. The owner, a farmer, had used it to store seed corn, and the vitriol mixture with which the seed corn was sprayed had dyed some of the stone flagstones blue. The cottage had no electricity, no water and no drainage. The price was £400, which I borrowed from Lorna Lewis. There was a well, which doubled as a refrigerator, and a hand pump in the kitchen. I had oil lamps and a huge log fire. I cooked by calor gas and a local builder mended the roof and constructed a septic tank.

To reach Willows I had to drive across a grass field. Arriving home one Friday night after dark, I found, as I bumped my way homewards, headlights dimmed in accordance with government regulations, that a stack had been built on the track, and the muddy ground had been churned up by the tractors. In a moment my car was stuck. I had to carry my suitcase for the rest of the way and get a tow in the morning.

Later, when petrol was scarcer, I used to bicycle to the nearest station, Clanfield. It was the friendliest and most informal of stations. One day I arrived late and to my horror saw the London train pulling out of the station. I yelled and waved, flung my bicycle down on the bank by the station entrance and ran. The kind engine driver stopped and I got on. Some other kind friend, probably the Station Master, rescued my bike and it was waiting for me when I returned home several days later. No one thought anything of it.

My late sister Nita's staff visited me with some concern for the primitive conditions in which I was living and Farish, the chauffeur, told me there was a disused old cast-iron boiler standing in one of Tiddington's sheds. He suggested he should bring it over. A few days later he and the cook and the housemaid, Blackie and Ethel, both of whom had worked for my mother for some thirty years, duly arrived with the boiler in the back of the Buick. They also brought my sister's needlework box which was a present from my niece. They had filled it with sweets. The boiler was installed and I was able to have a hot bath.

Once the Second World War came to an end, people turned their thoughts to planning a better world. There were Royal Commissions on rural development, there was the exciting Beveridge Plan for Social Security, and, for the first time, a National Health Service. It was my job to break down the intricacies of these plans into a form that our W.I. members would find easier to digest. We spoke of the new idea of village colleges and discussed the adult education schemes of other countries, such as Denmark. My chairman, Adeline Vernon, and I talked of the possibility of some such college one day in the far future for the W.I. members. At one conference our speaker, Sir Richard Livingstone, described the Danish adult education scheme and during the lunchbreak Adeline Vernon suggested I should ask him to put forward our ideas for a college in his afternoon speech. He willingly agreed and the audience was surprised but wholly welcoming to the idea that one day W.I.s might have a college of their own. So was born the idea of Denman College, which I would come to head as Warden a few years later.

Towards the end of the war I began to think I should practise what I had preached among our members and take part in the local government. I consulted an old friend at the Home Office who had known me in my prison service days, Irene Wall. She said emphatically, "You should stand for Parliament." So I gave my name to the Labour Party Headquarters and shortly after heard from the Regional Officer for Suffolk, Miss Francis, who had read my book on prisons, "They Always Come Back." Next time I went to Bury St. Edmunds, Suffolk, on W.I. business I went to see her, and in due course was selected as a candidate. Although the date of the next general election had not been fixed, the N.F.W.I. thought that adoption as a candidate would be incompatible with my work, and when the general election day was announced, they terminated my appointment in 1945. At that time Lady Denman was chairman of the Women Liberals, the chairman of the Organisation Committee was a Labour candidate, and several W.I. executive committee members took a prominent part in their local Tory organisations. But the Staff was held to a different standard, and I left.

The war ended, a general election was called, and I fought my first election battle and lost. Then I had to look for a job.

The Oxford Worker's Education Association offered me work as a lecturer, but it was barely a living. Then the Association of Psychiatric Social Workers asked if I would be their Services After Care Officer in East Anglia, based in Cambridge. So I sold Willows sadly and moved to Cambridge. But my work covered Norfolk and I wanted to work in Suffolk, where the Labour Party had again chosen me as their parliamentary candidate. With the start of the National Health Service there was a wide demand for qualified psychiatric social workers, and I was appointed as the first social worker to St. Audry's Hospital, Melton near Woodbridge. I moved to a house in my own constituency, West Suffolk.

St Audry's was an old mental hospital with 1,000 beds in locked wards and a medical staff of three. The Medical Superintendent had a golf handicap of three, so he spent most of his day on the golf course. He took his morning ward round at a quick trot and if I wanted to see him that day I had to run with him and keep running. He gave me every facility, an office, a secretary and a completely free hand, but there were no amenities in the hospital, no canteen, not even a tea stall, no visiting library, no freedom at all for patients and no pocket money for them because it had never been anybody's job to apply. My secretary and I made out the hospital's first full list of patients, and to their intense astonishment, the old men got pocket money for smokes and the old ladies a lesser sum for sweets.

Given the Medical Director's rare presence, the hospital was virtually run by the Deputy Medical Officer, who was tireless, and by a devoted band of male and female nurses.

Within two years of my arrival new medical staff were appointed as well as a new and enterprising hospital secretary. He soon made many changes, much to the benefit of the hospital as a whole. A new canteen was built, wards were at last unlocked, and occupational therapy was improved and extended to many more patients.

When I had been at St. Audry's for six years, my niece in South Africa invited me to stay with her for three months. It was a wonderful opportunity, not to be missed. I asked if I could have sabbatical leave but this was refused. Hoping that it would not be difficult to get another job on my return, I gave in my notice and left for a wonderful holiday in Cape Town, Johannesburg, and what was then Rhodesia.

From December 1955 to March 1956 I was the guest of my niece and her husband, who was at the time a member of the South African parliament. I was able to attend a session at the Cape Town parliament, a great privilege, although my ignorance of Afrikaans was a severe draw-back. Looking down from the gallery I was struck by the dark complexions of the Members, descendants of Dutch settlers. This was the country where mixed marriages were banned. Yet a newcomer was left wondering about the mixed blood of the forebears of some of the sitting members.

My niece took me to one of the Game Reserves, where

we stayed two nights. We saw the footprints of a herd of elephants which had very recently passed that way. I was told that a small car had been flattened by a herd which had not bothered to deviate from its route. So our car was hastily turned round.

We saw a lioness pick up her loitering cub and carry him unhurriedly across the road to the cover beyond. We saw a large family of warthogs scurrying along in single file.

After Christmas my niece's family moved to their ranch near Gwanda, in what was then Rhodesia, for a carefree two weeks. Accommodation consisted of several rondaveks, each with its own bedroom, bath and W.C., and one larger building for sitting and eating. My niece and some of their guests did most of the cooking, but all domestic chores, including washing-up, were done by local residents recruited by the South African wife of the ranch manager. He and his wife and small boy came to dinner one night and I asked the little boy about the injured eagle which had been caught a few days before and was now surprisingly caged in with a few odd hens in the farmyard, convalescing.

"How did you catch him?" I asked the little boy, thinking of the bird's lethal talons, which were only too apparent. "Did you wear gloves?"

"We don't wear gloves in Rhodesia," was the scornful reply.

Back in Johannesburg I visited Soweto. I drove through some of the monotonous streets and sat in on a baby clinic. From the raised ground on which stood the visitors' café, built for whites only, I looked over the hundreds of identical houses and identical streets. It was a very depressing sight.

I also visited gold mines and diamond mines and saw the grading of priceless gems. It seemed a world apart.

Back home and back to everyday life I decided I would

not hurry to get a job. With the £20 I had won betting on my niece's horse at the Cape Town races I bought a white poodle puppy and planned to breed her. A few years later, thanks to her litters, I enjoyed a motoring trip in Holland and a holiday in France.

I also bought two goats, intending to sell milk and cheese, and I planned to sell vegetables on the nearest W.I. market stall. While these plans were still churning over in my mind, another dearly loved relative rang me to say that her eldest daughter, eighteen and unmarried, was pregnant. There were two younger sisters at school and they lived in a small village. The young woman's father had been retired from the services on psychiatric grounds. What to do with her?, my relative asked me. Had I any suggestions?

In 1956 such a situation was looked on in a very different way from today. I replied that I was temporarily unemployed and that the young woman, whom I hardly knew, should stay with me till we could sort things out.

A week later a forlorn little figure in a heavy overcoat much too big for her arrived on my doorstep. I gave her my bedroom and moved up to the attic. She stayed with me till it was time to go to the maternity home. Her father, who had not been consulted in the early stages, paid me £2. 10 shillings a week for her keep

The villagers, although I was a newcomer, were wonderfully supportive. The W.I. secretary asked us both to tea, and became a good friend. The vicar, an ex-Ghurka colonel, and his whole family also were most helpful.

I enlarged my livestock and bought three Chinese geese. I built a new garage from hollow breeze blocks; the only assistance I had came from a neighbour who helped me lift the corrugated iron sheets onto the roof.

The young woman was totally ignorant of housework,

cooking, gardening or the care of animals, but gradually she took on a few odd jobs.

When the goslings were hatched, not knowing their sex we called them Marshall and Snelgrove. Because of the unpredictable behaviour of their father, we reared them in the linen cupboard. Marshall and Snelgrove did more than I could to distract a very unhappy adolescent from her near-total self-absorption.

It was nearly at the end of her stay with me that I had an unexpected letter from the superintendent of St Andrew's Hospital, Thorpe, near Norwich. I had known him when I was doing After Care for ex-Service psychiatric patients after I left the W.I.s in 1945. Dr. McCulley wrote to offer me the post of psychiatric social worker. The fifty-mile daily drive from Suffolk to Thorpe should present no problems, he said. Idiotically, I believed him. Six months later, now on my own, I sold my Suffolk house and its livestock, except for the poodle, and bought a bungalow in East Carleton, five miles from Thorpe.

The forlorn eighteen-year-old, her baby adopted, was slowly rebuilding her life. She came to Norfolk to train as a nurse. While she lived in the hospital, she and her friends were frequent visitors at my bungalow. She qualified and later married, and I was proud of her success.

# CHAPTER 10

# Denman College

Betty Christmas always described herself to her fellow
W.I. organisers as the village girl who made good. She had
worked in the village post office when she left school, then
learnt shorthand and typing and rose to be W.I. County
Secretary. She was delighted at being made a national
general organiser and she was much loved by her fellow
organisers and all W.I. members who came in contact with
her. Although she was not a member of the National
Federation Education Sub-Committee she often attended
and from the first was a supporter of our plans for
establishing some kind of W.I. educational college after
the war. Together she and I drew up the first blueprint, and
this was presented to the Executive by my chairman, Mrs.
Vernon. Its success, we knew, depended on the reactions
of Lady Denman. Lady Denman listened gravely and then
said, "Do you think anyone would come?" Mrs. Vernon
and others soon persuaded her that W.I. members *would*
come, and that this was was really an extension of the day
schools and conferences we had already been holding, plus
an opportunity for craft classes and cookery, and a wonderful cheap four-day holiday for countrywomen who
could seldom afford to get away from their livestock, their
families, and their daily chores.

I had already left the W.I. when finally a house was
bought and the college opened in 1948. It was named after

Lady Denman, who had died two years earlier. Betty was the obvious choice as Warden; I doubt if any other applicant was even considered.

Betty's charm and her welcoming smile made a success of the college from the start. There were considerable difficulties as well. W.I. students arrived on Monday evening and left on Friday morning. No weekend courses were offered and the college closed down for all of August and part of September, and for Christmas and Easter. Because it was felt that as many W.I. members as possible should be given the chance of attending a course, priority was given to members from W.I.s which had not previously sent anyone. This meant delaying the members' confirmation of acceptance until only a short time before the course was held. As a result, many W.I.s soon gave up trying for places, which at first were always overbooked. The consequence of these practises was that many of the courses eventually ran at a loss.

Tragically Betty developed cancer. There were spells in hospital and for many sad months Betty lay on her bed in the sitting room of the Warden's cottage. But she refused to give up the reins and no one had the temerity to suggest she should. The college was her life. One of the staff told me that although Betty insisted on having the files kept under her bed, she was no longer capable of going through the applications. I used to visit her from time to time and it was heartrending to see her, surrounded by a worshipping staff, and a few carefully selected W.I. members, and quite incapable of administering anything.

More hospitalisation followed and on one of my visits Betty asked me if I could find her a white poodle puppy, like mine, which she could give as a Christmas present to her brother. Like all her friends, I couldn't refuse her anything.

Back home in Norfolk, after much searching I at last

heard of a poodle litter and went to choose one. I arranged with Betty that her brother should meet me at the hospital to collect the puppy. Early one cold December morning I set out in snow to pick up the puppy in Cromer and then drive the 150 miles to the hospital. The puppy slept peacefully, nursed by my own poodle bitch. When I got to the hospital I tucked the pup under my sheepskin coat and when Betty saw its little woolly head peering out she burst into tears. Mercifully her brother, in spite of snowy roads, arrived shortly afterwards.

It was a few months after Betty died that I had a letter from the Denman staff. Would I consider taking Betty's place? This was followed by a letter from Lady Dyer, the N.F.W.I. chairman, to the same effect.

I still had a pensionable job at St. Andrew's Hospital, Thorpe, near Norwich. I had a house, two poodles, three Chinese geese and a garden. I was quite content with my life. But I had helped to give birth to Denman College and I knew that after Betty's long illness they were in trouble. I went down to see them and was persuaded.

So I sold my house, and for the first time after many house movings, I made a loss on it. Still, what did it matter? I would be at Denman until I retired and I could transfer my pension.

I moved into a different Warden's Cottage and Betty's Warden's cottage was turned into student accommodation. My cottage was cold, dark and damp and some of my books and framed photos bear mildew marks to this day. But I was propelled by the hope that Denman could be restored to play an active part in W.I. life. It struck me at once that it was hopelessly uneconomic for the college to close every weekend, for some two months during summer and for a fortnight at Christmas and Easter. When I arrived, student vacancies were sometimes filled at the last moment from the Bursar's secret list of elderly W.I.

members who were lonely or lived by themselves and were wiling to take up such vacancies at short notice regardless of their suitability for the course, or indeed for residential accommodation. One, I found out, lovable and slightly confused, was incontinent, for example, though I was assured that she was such a dear old thing that she couldn't be refused. The staff were deeply shocked when I suggested a waterproof sheet.

While W.I. members raised large sums for the college, they were not allowed to visit it except during two weeks in August when the place was empty. Even if a W.I. member was going to be on holiday in the neighbourhood and called asking if she could look round she was turned away. I was horrified, and one of my first suggestions was that the college should be open to all W.I. members whenever they wanted to visit, provided they gave advance notice.

"Who would show them round?" asked my startled staff.

"I would show them round," I replied. For the first six months of this new practise we were flooded with visitors, and then, as was to be expected, the visits tailed off.

Denman College staff consisted of the warden, a bursar and a college secretary – Christine and Barbara, both W.I. members of long standing – and a tutor, Delphine, who was responsible for engaging speakers and, during Betty's long illness, for planning courses. She kept a meticulous card index of speakers' names and addresses which I found invaluable on my appointment. Mrs. Flanders was the secretary who typed all our letters. A German married to an Oxford tutor, she used to arrive punctually each morning on a Messerschmidt scooter. Her English was impeccable and when she returned a letter to me saying the meaning was unclear I always knew that I was wrong and she was right.

There was a cook and usually two kitchen maids, found, and at intervals replaced, by a cookery school seeking practical experience for its students.

The college's outside staff consisted of a gardener and a steward. The housework was done by an army of "dailies" under the supervision of the housekeeper.

Denman College is a beautiful house, built in 1820 and standing in 100 acres, part of which forms "The Wilderness." There were in 1958 two additional residences, the Old and the New Croft, and altogether, accommodation for about forty-five students. Each bedroom had been furnished by a different county federation and the W.I. members, who had also given generously to the purchase, were justly proud of their lovely handmade quilts, curtains, bedcovers and cushions with which the rooms were furnished. My office on the first floor was a particularly charming room, with a beautiful view across the lawn to the lake. Every morning it gave me fresh pleasure when I opened the door to begin the day.

The college offered a wide range of classes, from astronomy (taught by Patrick Moore) to heraldry, from Cotswold history to French wines, from social legislation (at which Lord Beveridge generously took the chair) to patchwork. There were classes in every kind of handicraft, in domestic science (with practical sessions conducted in the new domestic science wing) and in music and painting. Tuition fees ranged from 15 shillings for a weekend course (an innovation I introduced) to £2 for a full Monday-Friday week.

We were fortunate in having so many well-known and distinguished lecturers, as well as rising young artists, like David Gentleman, who accepted our invitation to come to Denman.

It seemed to me that my task was to get the college going again after its months of retreat from reality during Betty's long illness. So after we had established a first-come-first-served method of application and the occasional weekend courses, I initiated three courses which were at the time considered completely revolutionary: a weekend course for husbands and wives; a three-day course for mothers and babies; and a family weekend. For the married couples' weekend we conducted the usual programme of some three or four simultaneous courses. For the family weekend we had a reduced choice but we provided childrens' beds, some cots, some tents and a playground in the garden, which was manned by volunteer Marcham W.I. members, a Guide Captain and other kind supporters. All were much appreciated.

Because the college had been under-used for so long, funds were low. In order to make money some of our flower arranger demonstrators organised a Flower Arrangers' Exhibition (opened by Constance Spry); 42 county federations took part, and we made a profit of £700, a highly satisfactory sum in those days. It also offered an opportunity to W.I. members to come and see their college and this they did with pleasure.

I bought a camera and took coloured slides of college rooms and current classes and we packaged this set of slides and offered them, for a modest hire fee (10/6d.) to any W.I. who wanted to show them at their monthly meeting. Some of the slides were used in the history of the W.I. movement which replaced the book I had written about the movement during the war, published as part of the Collins "Britain in Pictures" series.

In an abrupt and troublingly unfair dismissal on the part of our N.F.W.I. employers, our tutor Delphine was replaced by a younger Oxford graduate. Geraldine was hardworking and invariably cheerful; she was a great asset to the staff, who sadly missed Delphine. When I took up my appointment as Warden, some of the staff did not find it easy to adjust to the quickened pace of life after having been used to much more free time. With hindsight I think I tried to change too much too quickly. Because the new year-round schedule meant that staff leave now had to be taken, as in other places of employment, in rotation, some particularly resented both the schedule and the intrusion of visiting W.I. members.

There was also Sam, a lovable elderly black labrador, who had been a present to Betty from Lady Brunner. Endearingly, Sam thought he owned Denman. He was there to welcome new arrivals, he had free range of the college and he slept on any upholstered chair and on any quilted bed if the bedroom door had been left open. I protested that, however endearing, he could not be allowed to ruin priceless quilts. And I protested at his smell. Christine was not at all pleased at any criticism (hadn't he been "dear Betty's" dog?), but agreed to take him to a vet. When she was on sick leave she took him home to live with her.

In June 1958, after an absence of some weeks, Christine returned to half-time duties but was clearly not at all well. On doctor's advice she later gave in her notice and retired. She had never disguised her opposition to any change from the routine of "dear Betty."

One day in the autumn Lady Dyer (the N.F.W.I. chairman) paid us a visit, and I walked round the gardens with her and showed her the avenue of young red oaks, donated by the Canadian W.I.s, which we had all taken turns in weeding. When I had arrived they were smothered in long grass and a few of the trees had died. Now they were flourishing and we were proud of them.

"I don't know how you have done so much in such a short time," said Lady Dyer.

A few weeks later I had a telegram early one morning from a W.I. Executive member, Peg Ransome, a personal friend and treasurer of Norfolk W.I.s, saying, "All my support and love. Good luck." I had no idea what it meant. But when the post arrived there was a letter from Lady

Dyer asking for my resignation, and saying she would visit Denman in two days' time. She arrived and presented me with a letter, signed by herself, terminating my employment. I was dumbfounded and asked why. She said there was a "staff crisis," that my administration was hopeless and that the Executive had decided I must go. Later I learnt that she had in her handbag an alternative letter accepting my resignation if I had agreed. I did not, and I told Lady Dyer I would consult a solicitor. The terms of my dismissal gave me twelve days to hand over the office and three weeks to clear out of the Warden's cottage After the twelve days I was forbidden to set foot inside the college except with written permission from Lady Dyer.

If I had defrauded the college or been found in bed with the gardener, the terms of dismissal could hardly have been more insulting. Letters of protest came pouring in from W.I.s and other dismayed supporters, but the decision stood.

I was sacked apparently largely on allegations made by the two Bursars, Christine and the current Bursar, who shortly afterwards resigned because she admitted her duties were beyond her capabilities in spite of having been given an assistant to do the accounts. According to Lady Dyer, I was sacked for "lack of administrative experience." I was, she wrote, "a square peg in a round hole." Yet I had halved the college deficit in a year and doubled the intake of students, thereby enabling the National Federation to ask for an increased grant from the Ministry of Education, which came through the week I left Denman.

A nice final touch to my dismissal was that the N.F.W.I. sent me, four months after I had been turned out, a payment of £23 2s. 7d. "in lieu of board at the rate of 35s. 7d. a week for thirteen weeks." I gave the money to the Norfolk W.I.s as they had been so wonderfully supportive, and they bought some chairs with it.

97

# Supporting Recovered Mental Patients: Norfolk and Norwich Association for Mental Health

I was fifty-eight with no home, no job and an unexplained, unexplainable slur on my character. But my friends were wonderful. My friend Dorothy took me in for Christmas and even though she was no dog lover, accepted my pregnant poodle as well. Later Mary Duff found me temporary accommodation in Dunston, Norfolk, and within a few weeks the Norfolk Chief Education Officer offered me a job. It was indeed most welcome. It took time for me to recover my balance.

I remained with the Norfolk Child Guidance team until I was offered another Child Guidance Clinic job in Hertfordshire. This had more scope and involved work with a bigger team. While I worked there, I lived with my niece in Amwell, Hertfordshire, from Monday to Friday and returned home to Dunston for the weekend.

In 1964, four years late, I qualified for my retirement pension. (The delay was due to my early employment abroad, when I had not contributed to National Insurance.) With no clear ideas about future plans I decided to give up my job at the Hertfordshire Child Guidance Clinic and come home to Norfolk and have time to read, to look after the garden and to enjoy some leisure. So I thought.

A few weeks later Edith Botting, my successor as social worker at St. Andrew's Hospital, Norwich, came to see me and said she thought Norfolk ought to start a branch of the National Mental Health Association. Would I arrange a meeting where people interested in social work, and in particular, mental health, might meet and discuss this?

About twelve people came to a meeting held in my house which was chaired by Edith. We had representatives from the County Social Services and from Norwich City Hall, from the Red Cross, the Women's Voluntary Services, British Legion, W.I.s, Rotary and various other voluntary bodies. It was unanimously agreed that although mental handicap was covered by the Norfolk Society for Mentally Handicapped Children, no agency covered the field of mental health and no organisation provided a back-up for the two big psychiatric hospitals. It was therefore decided to form a new voluntary body affiliated to the national body now called "MIND."

Edith, who had kept this particular card up her sleeve, then said to me, "As you are retired and have nothing to do, Cicely, you had better be Honorary Secretary." This was agreed.

Edith asked for a contribution from all present to cover our new group's initial expenses, and suggested half a crown each. So with the princely sum of thirty shillings, I was left to launch this new society.

Twenty-five years later, the Norfolk and Norwich Association for Mental Health has a paid staff of twenty-five, and in 1989 its expenditure was £271,000. Today there are seven Norfolk branches (expenditure £230,000 in 1989), a Norwich short-term hostel of thirty beds and several day centres and sheltered workshops for younger ex-patients.

99

Such has been the sequel to those first twelve contributions of half a crown!

In 1965, shortly after our launching, I approached the two mental hospitals in Norfolk. In the first, the medical superintendent said he would give all the help he could. The reply from the other was more cautious. He would wait and see, he said.

The two local authorities reacted similarly. The County was most encouraging and within a short time gave us a yearly contribution of £10. Norwich City was more cautious of this new-fangled idea, and after some delay, gave us £5 a year.

Our objectives were to make the public more aware of the problems of mental illness and to offer help and friendship to discharged patients returning to their homes. The hard-pressed County Welfare Officers, whose duties included after-care, welcomed our badly needed help.

At that time, in the 1960s, twenty years after the launching of the National Health Service, mental illness was still looked upon by the average citizen as something to be feared, probably incurable, and totally incomprehensible. It was not unusual that one of our new members, on being asked if she would be willing to drive a long-term patient from St. Andrew's Hospital to visit her family a few miles outside Norwich, inquired fearfully, "Is her illness catching?" Even with the support of another less fearful member, she was reluctant to share a car with a mental patient.

To help educate an interested but ignorant general public, we organised lectures in Norwich by experts on subjects such as schizophrenia, after-care of mental patients, and depression. Admission was free but there was a collection plate at the door. All the lectures were well-attended and the collection invariably covered our costs: speaker's fee, the hiring of the room and postage. Looking

100

back on those early days of our newly formed association, it is astonishing to me that well-known university professors such as Peter Townshend, and medical superintendents of large psychiatric hospitals were willing to come to address our struggling group. All we did was cover their expenses and pay them a paltry fee. We were deeply indebted to their generosity in giving up their time and sharing their knowledge.

One of our speakers was Dr. Richard Fox, then Medical Superintendent of Severall's Hospital, Colchester. He showed slides of the newly opened Essex Group Home, where five women recovered, former mental patients, lived together with no resident supervision. They were responsible for their own housekeeping. This was the first scheme of its kind in the country.

Shortly after Dr. Fox's lecture one of Norfolk's welfare officers, George Brown, came to see me to suggest that our infant association should start a similar scheme. Over a cup of coffee he and I drew up a budget, which he jotted down on the back of his cigarette packet. With a copy of this I went to my somewhat incredulous committee and surprisingly they agreed to launch a Group Homes scheme if the hospitals agreed. Once more, one Medical Superintendent, Dr McCulley of St Andrew's Hospital, agreed to participate while the other preferred to wait and see.

At St Andrew's Hospital the work of choosing possible group home residents was delegated to a young psychiatrist, Dr Neale. In the face of considerable scepticism from the nursing staff and some of the medical staff, but with the backing of Dr McCulley, Dr Neale selected six women patients as candidates for training. Their ages ranged from fifty-eight to seventy-five. One had been in hospital continuously and without even one day's home leave for the last thirty-seven years – more than half her life. Two had

101

been hospitalised for twenty years each. Two were diagnosed as schizophrenic, three as depressives and one as epileptic. The six, later reduced to five, were brought from different wards and were told that they were going to attend classes in cooking and housekeeping. Some of the ward staff were intrigued by the new scheme and others were openly antagonistic and thought it all a lot of nonsense.

"They are happy here in hospital," one of the medical staff said to me. "Why do you want to upset them?" Nurses would shake their heads and say, "They will never make it outside."

But Dr Neale persisted and Margaret Murray, Occupational Therapist, gave unstinting support. I attended regular discussion meetings with prospective residents, who were silent and fearful.

Meanwhile, we went house-hunting and the chairman of our association, Mr C. Kevill Davies, most generously offered to guarantee a £2,000 bank loan for the project. His faith in our infant enterprise was remarkable and it was his generosity that made the scheme viable.

We bought a house in Norwich for £1,650. We decorated it ourselves: the Townswomen's Guild gave us curtain material, W.I.s all over Norfolk gave us china and furnishings, and Norfolk firms supplied beds and bed linen for nothing or for absurdly low sums. I toured the county telling meetings about our new venture and asking them to collect surplus household goods which I could collect on my return, say a month later. People contributed odd cups, kitchen ware that didn't match, and carpet lengths of varying sizes, but put together it all made a home.

At last came the day when we could say to our class of five, "Come and see your new home." They were appalled at this news.

"We can't leave hospital," they said. "Who would look after us?"

They said all the things that the most pessimistic members of staff had said they would say. It was depressing. All our preparation appeared to have been in vain.

So I asked them to come and have tea in their new house. Reluctantly, and accompanied by a helpful Sister, they arrived one afternoon in a hospital ambulance. Five depressed old ladies – their names were Nellie, Violet, Hilda, Dolly and Daisy – filed into the sitting room and slumped into armchairs, silent and unsmiling. When they looked at the coal fire burning brightly in the grate there was a flicker of interest, a half smile but no more.

I walked down the corridor to the kitchen to make tea and they watched lugubriously. Then Nellie's head lifted and her eyes brightened.

"It's a *teapot*!" she said in amazement.

It was the first time for thirty years that she had had tea out of teapot and not out of a metal urn built for fifty cups.

That did it.

"Could we make tea when we liked?" Violet asked, greatly daring.

"Could we have butter sometimes, not marge?" Dolly asked.

Then the awful, imponderable problems overwhelmed them again. Who would manage the housekeeping money? Who would choose the food they ate? We had been through it before a hundred times, but they were very frightened. Nellie, we told them once again, was to be the housekeeper. She would take 30/-a week from each resident and each would pay the rent collector (one of our Committee) £1 a week rent. They would each have their pensions.

But would they get *all* their old age pension? they asked. ALL? The hospital had always kept back most of it. And could they have a four-minute boiled egg, boiled by themselves in a saucepan and not in a net with fifty others?

103

Life's possibilities were opening up beyond their dreams. They returned to the hospital.

After the tea party they came to the house several times again, nominally to help me with the final touches. In fact, they were almost totally useless at the time because, as they said, Sister had told them they must never stand on a chair in case they felt giddy. So hanging curtains was out. Nor could they plug or unplug an electric light fitting, nor touch the bulb. Such hazards might be fatal, Sister had warned them.

Then came the day on which they moved in. A week later I pointed out that the clock wanted winding.

"Sister always did that," they replied.

I said that the flowers I had arranged for them the previous week were now quite dead, couldn't they be thrown out?

"But *you* put them there," they protested, perplexed. "We didn't like to move them." So they had been dusted and the dead stalks carefully put back in their vases.

Cooking too was a daily hazard. After twenty years in hospital the residents had forgotten whether you boiled potatoes for an hour or two minutes. Daisy, our most adventurous resident, had last lived in a normal world when she was in her early twenties – that was in the days before nylon, before frozen peas and fish fingers and before plastic was invented. Greatly daring, when it was her turn to help in the kitchen she made a blackberry and apple pie, and cooked it in a plastic dish. That taught her about plastics. Daisy also ironed her first-ever nylon stockings. That taught her about nylon.

For the first six months Daisy tried out her new-found freedom in many highly original ways. She was fifty-eight, and she bought a miniskirt, but unfortunately had not heard of tights. It was her fellow residents who pointed out the gaps.

She also bought necklaces and bangles, earrings and brooches and piercingly vivid red lipstick and purple eyeshade. Her grey hair suddenly became a flaming red. She bought a sewing machine in the market and then found there was no needle, and no available needle would fit it. Daisy learnt the hard way, but she remained undaunted.

She bought a bicycle and bicycled the twenty miles to Yarmouth. It was the first time she had bicycled for thirty-seven years. Arriving at Yarmouth she put it on a train and came home, exhausted but triumphant.

The residents were extraordinarily tolerant of each other's ways and particularly if one of them suffered from depression. This was something they knew about and could sympathise with. But if one of them had a common cold or diarrhoea, they had no sympathy and no idea how to cope with it nor willingness to try.

"Sister looked after anyone who was ill," they would say curtly. "It's not our responsibility."

So when Violet, the oldest, rather frail resident, had a stomach upset, they gave her fried sausage, fried bread and Ovaltine and were surprised and resentful when she was sick. No one thought of a hot water bottle.

Before the group home was opened our Committee had discussed what we should tell its neighbours. We decided truth was best. So I visited the little grocer and general store which stood on the other side of the street and also our two immediate neighbours. All were most helpful. All of them had some distant or close relative who had suffered from mental breakdown. The shopkeeper was particularly kind in helping our residents check change (they had rarely handled money and had no idea of prices) and helped them too with the new delight of telephoning relatives from the call box.

Two years later, when we opened our fourth group home, our residents became the Universal Aunts of the neighbourhood. They acted as babysitters, as dog sitters and even, at the request of a worried husband, checked that his depressed wife took her tablets at the right time and in the right quantity.

"We know about tablets," said our residents cheerfully.

Within five years our first group home was self-supporting and we had repaid the loan.

The history of group homes is in many ways the history of the development of modern psychiatric treatment and the public reaction to it. Our first residents might have come off a desert island for all they knew of current daily life. So utterly ignorant were they of modern gadgets that a gas cooking stove, a Hoover, and a fridge were all new techniques with unforeseen hazards to be mastered the hard way. It was months before our first residents would accept that a gas cooker with a pilot light did not need a match.

Similarly, to be accepted in the community was an unexpected and delightful experience for them. The local church was helpful, and the all too frequent rejection by their families was accepted with sadness and surprisingly little resentment. Once I took Daisy to see her brother and sister-in-law, who lived on a prosperous chicken farm within easy distance of Norwich. She had not seen them for over twenty years. They had never visited her in the hospital. They agreed to our visit reluctantly, but made Daisy pay for the half dozen eggs she brought away with her and never visited or enquired about her afterwards, though she wrote to them and loved her brother dearly.

Our second group home, opened a year after the first, was already less of a totally different environment from hospital. Three of the residents had contacts with family that they had maintained in hospital, though one had a daughter who persistently refused to see her. This group adapted to shared household responsibility more quickly than the first, and with far less friction.

106

Moreover this second home was a Council house leased to us by the city local authority that had had a change of heart. (Gone were the days when the housing authority did not, on principle, rehouse recovered mental patients.)

Our third group home was for men, and it was donated by the Lions Club. The hospital's male nursing staff had done very little to prepare the men for independent living, and the new residents had few, if any, household skills. But they were better at looking after the garden, and neighbours, expecting men to be helpless in the house, soon rallied round.

Within ten years we had mixed group homes for men and women, and the bedrooms became bed-sitting rooms, each with their own key. Hospital patients by that time were used to having greater freedom than in the past and after a much shorter time than our first residents, no longer feared going out alone and were no longer totally ignorant of modern gadgets.

In the early days of the group homes we had no paid staff. I was the Honorary Secretary and when we opened our first home I visited every day for the first week, then less regularly, as it seemed necessary. Our voluntary rent collector, a Committee member, visited once a week.

Two years or so after we launched the Norfolk and Norwich Association for Mental Health it was decided I should be paid an honorarium, and we settled for half a psychiatric social worker's salary. When we opened our third group home we appointed a part-time paid social worker, an American, who found Norfolk voices as great a problem as our residents found her New York voice. But they liked her friendliness. In 1972 we appointed a full-time paid Organising Secretary and in 1982, when Mr. Kevill Davies left Norwich, I was elected Chairman of the Association. I stayed on for the next eleven years, resigning in 1983.

The story of Daisy's final emancipation illustrates the change in official and public attitudes to former mental patients over the last twenty years.

Daisy had been thirty-seven years in hospital. After a year in our first group home, and now the owner of a working bicycle and a useless sewing machine, Daisy decided she would apply for a Council flat and meanwhile would move into lodgings on her own. Greatly daring, she took herself off to City Hall and put down her name on the waiting list. Then she found herself lodgings in a house which had fifteen other residents, one bathroom with a gas geyser on the first floor, and one W.C., usually blocked and unusable. She had an oil cooking ring in her furnished ground-floor room, but no water tap, either in her room or on the ground floor. The whole house was deplorable and so were the tenants. But it was one more step to independence.

When I heard of her housing application to the City I wrote to the Medical Officer of Health to back up her application, and enclosed a letter from the G.P. saying that she was fit to live alone. The Medical Officer of Health replied that his Council had never re-housed a mental patient and saw no reason why they should. Didn't I know they had a waiting list? I went to see him and stressed the need to help recovered mental patients, particularly now when hospitals had a more relaxed view about discharge. Modern drugs had made recovery possible, something not credible in the past. Ours, I said, was a new venture. Both the G.P. and myself, a qualified psychiatric social worker, considered Daisy fit to live by herself. The Medical Officer of Health (who had never met Daisy) shook his head. He would send one of his Housing Officers to investigate.

After some weeks, and many telephone calls from me, a Housing Officer visited Daisy in her lodgings. He asked her if her accommodation was self-contained. Daisy had no idea what this meant, so she said "Yes." The Officer returned to his department and struck her name off the waiting list. She was, he said, not in need of re-housing. When I did my regular telephone check-up I told him there was only one W.C. for fifteen inmates and that it was more often than not blocked. There was no water in her room and only one communal bathroom. Daisy's name was reinstated on the waiting list.

There was another long wait.

After more repeated telephone calls, the Housing Department sent a Sanitary Inspector to see Daisy. Rather unfortunately he arrived at the same time as Russell, Daisy's boy friend, a knife grinder whom she had met in the street when she was at our group home, and who became and remained her devoted friend for the next ten years. Russell, an elderly widower, told the Inspector there was no need to re-house Daisy as he was going to marry her. So her name was crossed off again.

Next time I saw Daisy I asked why she had let Russell tell the inspector she was going to marry him when she had no intention of doing so.

"Well, Miss McCall," said Daisy, "It was ever so awkward. There was Russell sitting there and I didn't like to say I wasn't going to marry 'im. It was ever so awkward." I could see her point.

So once again I went to the Housing Department and explained, and in a few weeks Daisy got her first flat, the first ex-certified mental patient in Norfolk to be rehoused. And there she remained, with daily visits from Russell, until fifteen years later, when she died.

Once I asked her why she didn't marry Russell.

"I got my freedom now," she replied. "Don't want no responsibilities."

Sometimes he slept in the house, sometimes he was kicked out and returned to his own Council flat. Like the

109

other group home residents, Daisy was wholly intolerant of physical illness. If Russell had a cough he could take it elsewhere. She wasn't going to put up with it, keeping her awake at night. If he had eczema on his hands he could go to the surgery and get them bound up. She hadn't time to bandage them. Maybe if he had hallucinated she would have been sympathetic; she would have understood that.

But always Russell came back and stayed till the next flare-up when he was sent packing. So he remained the faithful lover.

All those early group homes residents were inveterate collectors. After years with no possessions of their own, they bought useless baubles at jumble sales and church fêtes and on the Norwich market. Daisy filled her narrow corridor and her bedroom with piles of odd lengths of material, jumble clothes she never wore, useless bric-a-brac, never to be displayed.

One day Daisy told me she wanted a kitten, something of her very own, a loving companion. Together we went to the R.S.P.C.A. and brought back a furry bundle. It was all a kitten should be. A few weeks later she found its little body on the path between the shared gardens. It had been poisoned, deliberately, she thought. Did the stigma against recovered mental patients go as far as this?

While group homes expanded in Norfolk, the idea spread to other counties, and indeed other countries. I had many invitations to speak at meetings of other county mental health associations contemplating starting their own schemes. We had constant visitors and some of our committee members felt that our residents were becoming too much like exhibition specimens. But the residents were unperturbed and were proud to show off their housekeeping. Their new skills and learning were a matter of pride. They were well aware that their success could lead to the discharge of other long-term patients in other parts of the country.

110

In 1970 I was asked to do a tour of Ontario and, with our residents' permission, I took along a film made by the B.B.C. as well as coloured slides I had taken of the residents, including Daisy and her bicycle. Soon after I returned from Canada a group home was opened in Ottawa.

In 1973 I was awarded the M.B.E. for my work with group homes and our residents added a photograph taken outside Buckingham Palace to the collection of oddments on their mantelpiece. As I repeatedly told them, it was their efforts which had made the group home a success much envied and widely copied in other parts of the country and beyond. They were the ones who should have the medal.

They did not get a medal, but they did get a visit from Princess Alexandra, President of the National Association for Mental Health, who came and had tea with us. That was almost as good as going to Buckingham Palace, they decided.

# CHAPTER 12

# Dunston

In 1959, soon after I had moved into the Dunston bungalow so kindly lent me by its owner, my poodle, Judy,
produced four fluffy white puppies. They were a very
welcome diversion. One of them, Patsy, ultimately went to
the owner of the bungalow, a small return for her generosity to me, and was cherished by the four children who
shared her house.

One day, walking round the adjoining Dunston Hall
estate which had recently, with one exception, been sold in
separate lots to sitting tenants, I found a coachman's
cottage which appeared to be empty and so got in touch
with the estate agent. He told me this was now used as a
storehouse and therefore was not available, but he said
that there was a derelict plot of land on which I might be
able to get permission to build a house. Together we
trudged past the other half dozen houses of Dunston and
came to a ramshackle building with a corrugated iron roof
and at the end a small brick building which had housed the
electric motor and saw belt used on the estate. All round it
were nettles and brambles and odd piles of brick, cement
blocks and carved stone blocks for gate posts. It was a
dreary enough looking site, but the agent said that as the
saw bench had stood there for many years, permission
would not be difficult to get to build a house to replace it.

It was a bitterly cold February morning and our boots

squished in the mud. I turned away rather disconsolately. Then, on the other side of the track which ran through the plot, I saw a brick building with a massive chimney breast at one end. A green wooden tractor shed was attached at the far end. The remains of the builder's yard clutter surrounded it.

"What is that?" I asked.

"That," replied the agent, referring to his housing schedule, "is the Estate Yard and Workman's Bothy."

"But it must have been a house, with that great chimney," I said.

"No," replied the agent. "It is The Shed." And so, I learnt afterwards, was it known to local residents, and so indeed has it remained in the minds of many of them to this day.

But that brick chimney breast, I thought, that must be Tudor! I longed to see inside. It was locked. No one had the key, it seemed.

The nearest neighbour told me that the plot of land and the buildings had recently been sold but that he knew the buyer, who he said might be willing to consider an offer.

In due course I obtained a key, a massive eight-inch affair, and I opened the door and stepped into almost total darkness. On the opposite (north) wall were two windows, thick with dust. There were almost no windows on the south side. As my eyes got used to the dim light I saw at one end a massive Tudor fireplace with a huge bread oven beside it. The ceiling was some twenty feet high at the fireplace end and high up on the north side was another begrimed glazed and mullioned window. The rest of the ground floor, two thirds of the building, had a low ceiling, not much more than six feet high. There were massive oak beams. It was a sixteenth-century hall house.

I looked at the chimney breast, solid and serene, and felt very insignificant beside it. How many years of history had

113

it known? Four hundred, five hundred? How many families had baked bread in that great oven? Their red hot pokers had left scorch marks on the twelve-inch oak beam above.

Up the stairs was a bedroom with mullioned windows north and south. There was no glass, but there were marks where the shutters had been hooked back or slid to one side. Wooden shelves and pigeon holes lined one wall. On them lay piles of nails and iron hooks and hinges. The rest of the first floor was an open space, except for a halfway division which seemed to serve no purpose except to make the room even darker. The open space, later to become my second bedroom, had one back window, mullioned but unglazed. It was all incredibly dirty and totally dark.

A rough cut Tudor door led up to the attic. Here there were steep roof tiles lined with straw, and on one side three glass panels 18 inches by 12 inches, and a hole in the west end, a window which did not even have a frame. The east end was dominated by the brick chimney breast, rising to the sky.

Some of the floors still had the original wide planks, patched with later, narrower additions. The ground floor had little yellow bricks, laid on the bare earth.

In the middle of the ground floor stood an oak post, and against it an electric light bulb was draped incongruously at the end of a looped flex. It was the only light in the whole house. Along the south side there was a carpenter's bench and another bench stood at right angles near the electric light.

On the west end of the house was the paint shop. There were shelves round two walls and under the west window stood a slab of slate with smudges of red and blue paint.

Outside, amidst the clutter of old chimney pots, slabs of stone, and a forest of nettles, stood a three-seater privy. It had no partitions but it had a door.

114

I met the owner, who had bought the place a few weeks earlier from the Dunston Hall estate and intended to turn it into a store for second-hand tyres. I learnt later he had paid £250 for the buildings and the 2¼ acres that went with it. He sold it to me for £970. We both thought we had a bargain. It was only his future wife, whom he brought to see it after I had restored the house and garden, who felt he had missed his chance and told him so in no uncertain terms.

I was fortunate in having a wonderful architect. Wynne Thomas was the son-in-law of very old friends I had known in Cairo. I knew he had experience of restoring old houses. He never put a foot wrong.

I told him I had £2,000, the price I had got for my previous house, which I had sold when I went to Denman College. That had to cover everything, purchase price and repairs. It did.

Wynne drew up plans which would keep the original character of the house but let in light. I wanted underfloor heating because I though radiators would be obtrusive. I also wanted as much light as possible in the ground-floor sitting room. So we tore out the wooden boarding which formed the wall on the south side and demolished the tractor shed which leaned against it. We cut a hole in the second bedroom's south wall and put in a window so that it was no longer completely dark. With many gnawing doubts, we removed the mullions in the main bedroom and put in a casement window which could be opened.

We left the curious openwork dividing wall of the second bedroom but filled in the gaps. We cut a bit off to make a bathroom, and built solid partition walls.

Downstairs, the slate slab on which the paint had been mixed became my door step. We blocked up the window which looked straight into my neighbour's garden, and all along the south front of the sitting room we put windows, reaching from floor to ceiling and flooding the old beans with more light than they had seen since they stood as mighty trees in the forest.

Because it had been an estate yard there was plenty of building material lying to hand. I had the help of five wonderful friends and together we plastered all the inside walls and filled up holes, in some of them putting in the odd brick or stone, and leaving the professional builders to make good on the outside.

A six-foot carved stone which was propped up against one of the walls is now the kerb in front of the fireplace.

It was the moral support of my friends as much as their invaluable hard work that made the reconstruction possible. I could never have done it alone.

While mending holes in the bedroom walls I found that there was a continuous open space above the outside wall, just under the ceiling. This had provided much needed ventilation for the ground floor wood fire, which had supplied heating before the Tudor chimney was built. High up under the beamed ceiling of the twenty-foot-high end of the sitting room, a similar space had been provided at right angles to the chimney breast. It was not visible from the floor below, but the draught made its presence felt. Perhaps here had been the entrance for the swallow which had built its nest under the roof above the fireplace. The nest is still there.

I had seen the house first in February. On the first of April, still waiting for the final signing of documents, two friends and I knocked down the outside privy. It was a most satisfying act of total destruction. We attacked it with sledgehammers but we saved the old curved tiles, which matched the house tiles. Fortunately, the contract was duly signed the next day.

I fixed up a double extension flex to the one electric light fitting, and with Hoover in one hand and portable spotlight

116

in the other, I got rid of some of the dirt of many years. By this time I was working at the Child Guidance Clinic, so work had to be done in the evenings and at weekends.

I also had the help of Billie, a farm worker. He moved much of the clutter in the yard outside, stacked the stones and cut the nettles. One day I gave him two bucketfuls of nails collected from the pigeon holes which lined the walls of the principal bedroom. The pails were so heavy I could hardly lift them. He was delighted. Many were handmade, long and heavy. They would have lasted a lifetime. Unfortunately, Billie's life was to be a short one. He died only a year later. I often wondered what happened to that hoard of nails.

At the time I first discovered the hall house I explored the grounds, fighting my way through brambles and undergrowth. Turning a corner I came upon a moat, not something one expects to meet at the end of a garden. Had this, I wondered, been included in the plot of land that King John, so the records relate, had donated to his falconer together with the Manor of Dunston? The moat surrounded a small island on which now stood six tall pine trees. A narrow causeway provided access, and this was soon found by Judy the poodle as she burrowed her way through the brambles. Later she found she could slide down the lip of the island, and closely followed by Jill, the Jack Russell terrier, they would chase rabbits through the overhanging roots of the pine trees while I held my breath and waited for the fatal splash into the water beneath. Fortunately it never happened. They had a lovely time.

Perhaps, I thought, this island might have been where, in the Middle Ages, the Mother Superior lived with her sisterhood. Norwich Museum told me the island was probably inhabited up to the time of the Black Death, when Dunston, like so many Norfolk villages, was tragically almost depopulated.

117

I did not own the moat, but my boundaries came up to its edge. What an enchanting discovery to find on my first exploratory walk, pushing my way through the nettles!

I slept in the house for the first time on July 4th. Christian, my principal plasterer, joined me. Independence Day seemed a very suitable date to make the move. The next morning we were delighted to see the postman walking up to the front door.

"How did he know?" asked Christian.

But of course everyone in Dunston knew. And they all thought I was crazy to try and live in The Shed. Later I had a visit from George Nudd, who had worked as a carpenter at The Shed for fifty years.

"You won't have any trouble with that roof," he said. "I put the tiles on myself thirty years ago." It was reassuring.

George was amazed and delighted at the transformation. But he was disappointed that the wooden moulds for the Dunston lion's head, the crest of the former owners, the Longs, were no longer in the attic where he had left them. Hadn't I seen them, he asked querulously?

He gave me a manuscript, bound in disintegrating leather, and written by his grandfather, who had married the housekeeper at the Hall. It was a list of trees planted on the Dunston Hall estate between 1837 and 1840. Evidently there had been an afforestation plan and thousands of young trees had been planted, usually by "self and boy." (Once his grandfather had added pensively, "very wet day.") Hundreds of trees were "laid in graft," presumably heeled in, till self and boy had time to deal with them. Besides more usual trees, they planted a catalpa and a tulip tree and a "silver ash and silver fir." I asked a well-known nurseryman what these could be and he sent me two specimens, which now stand in my garden.

Now that the house was clean and habitable, I had time to

118

turn my attention to the garden. There was about an acre of snowberry, planted by the Longs of Dunston Hall for the pheasants. A neighbour provided a tractor and driver for one day and he demolished a large patch, but only too soon rooted seedlings appeared in profusion. Nita's sister-in-law, Dame Margery Corbett Ashby, came to help me, and on hands and knees, the two of us dug up every sprout. She was then in her late eighties; I was only sixty-two. She was a very dearly loved visitor who never came to stay with me without bringing her own gardening gloves. She would produce them from her luggage and say, disarmingly, "Where would you like me to begin?"

I also had the help of a group of university students. They organised a gang and together they waded into the pond and threw out the discarded rubbish of many ages. They found thick glass beer bottles, marked "1d." I rescued a glass inkwell, without its silver lining, but now in daily use as a flower vase. They also helped me to put up wire netting against the rabbits which infested the garden until I got a Jack Russell terrier. After that the rabbits kept a respectful distance.

Meanwhile I went to evening classes in woodwork and made my kitchen cupboards and formica working tops. The very kind instructor and a friend helped me to install them.

In the garden I found there were wild daffodils and snowdrops, and a few cowslips. I added to the bulbs each year as bit by bit I scythed down the nettles and brambles.

From holidays abroad I brought back further additions. There is now a six-foot chestnut, grown from a conker brought back from Versailles, and a sturdy Oregon Vine brought as a tiny cutting from Vancouver Island. Christian gave me an oak tree in a pot. It was an acorn she had planted in 1957. I planted it in 1959. Now it is a huge tree. Near to it stands a Paulownia, also grown in a pot on a

119

friend's kitchen window ledge from a seed she picked up in Chapelfield Gardens in Norwich. There are three walnut trees, given to me by the mother of one of my Child Guidance children.

I even made one commercial venture. I planted twenty-five baby Christmas trees for sale. But a coypu found them and after one night, more than half had their tops eaten. I dug them up and the local pest controller dealt with the coypus.

One of my early and best loved visitors to The End House was Rose Blackman – Blackie – who had been my mother's parlourmaid from as early as I can remember. As I noted earlier, together with Farish, Nita's chauffeur, and Ethel, formerly our housemaid, Blackie had provided my boiler at Willows. She was an important part of my life.

When our London house was sold, Blackie went to Nita as a cook, and Ethel, who had also been with my mother for some fifteen years, became Nita's housemaid. Ethel was the daughter of the Walmer stationmaster and joined the McCall household straight from school. She started as nursery maid and rose to be head housemaid. In our London house, when she first came to us, she used to take charge of the nursery when Wake, our nurse, had her day off. Ethel, then about fifteen, would play riotous games with Geoffrey and me. We would open the communicating doors between night nursery and day nursery and Wake's bedroom, and chase each other madly down the corridor. An added spice of excitement was that Wake would never have allowed such rowdiness, and certainly not on Sunday.

Ethel and Blackie loved each other dearly. But a new factor appeared when they moved to Nita's house and met Farish, Nita's chauffeur. He fell in love with Ethel and wanted to marry her. Blackie was emphatically opposed. No way would she allow this, and Ethel could not bear to disobey her. Yet all three remained devoted friends and for many years they would go away on holidays together, Farish driving for the two women. At first Nita and her husband lent them their car. Later Farish was helped to buy his own.

When Nita died in 1942, her house was sold. Ethel, Blackie and Farish, with help from the family, bought a house in Kilburn and for some time ran a small restaurant. Then Ethel developed cancer and died. Farish was heart-broken. His sister moved in to help run the house and Blackie, now in her eighties, became increasingly infirm.

Then Farish died. In his will he left the house to his sister and all his money to cancer research. Blackie had nothing but her pension and some savings.

I had visited them all at Kilburn from time to time. A few weeks after Farish's death his sister wrote to me to say she needed Blackie's room and could I find another accommodation for her. I had not seen Blackie for more than a year and was horrified when I visited and found her old and shaky and unwanted and confined to her first-floor bedroom. She had had a fall when she was out shopping and from that time had been too frightened to go out; there was a new fish and chip shop on the ground floor and they supplied her food. She had no contact with the social services, who indeed had never heard of her. I arranged for her to be visited and the social worker found her a place in an old people's home in Hertfordshire. With good food and loving care she soon improved, and I used to drive over from Dunston to pick her up and bring her back to The End House for a week's holiday. This was something of a strain on my housekeeping skills.

Before her visits I felt compelled to clean the silver and give windows and furniture an extra polish.

Helping me lay the table on the first visit, Blackie said somewhat testily, "I can't find the silver butter dish."

"I'm sorry Blackie, I haven't got one. I use a saucer."

"But what has happened to her Ladyship's butter dish?" she asked, bristling with disapproval.

I apologised and said humbly that I no longer had it. And I remembered the smart nimble parlourmaid of long ago, who never hesitated to use her abrasive wit on a little girl caught touching the dining room silver with sticky fingers. I apologised again for my fallen standards.

In the car on the three-hour journey from Hertfordshire to Dunston, Blackie would keep up a running commentary. She would read all the road signs, the names of the streets, and even of the shops. You might have thought there would be little to read in the open countryside but it was surprising what she found. "To let" signs, road directions, even "Keep out" signs were all read out aloud. Perhaps it was to show me she was missing nothing and was enjoying fresh sights.

On her visits to me I was always called "Miss Cicely" if we were alone. But when we had visitors I was promoted to "Miss McCall."

On the last night at the end of one of her visits I said, "I've got a treat for us. I've got a bottle of hock."

Unimpressed, she said primly, "Sir Robert always drank claret."

But she was far from being unappreciative. I had said one day that I hoped to buy a bird bath for the garden when I could afford it.

"I'll give you one," said Blackie. And she insisted on spending all her week's pension, £5, on a cement bird bath, which is still one of my most treasured possessions. A year later she died peacefully in the home. I still miss her.

Many years after I had returned The Shed to its original use, as a family home, I applied to have it listed. It is now Grade II, like most of the other houses in our little village. Dunston is Green Belt, and hopefully will remain so.

Thanks to the researches of a local historian, I now know

more of the house's past history. A yeoman farmer called Hudd lived in it for some years in the sixteenth century. He was a tenant of the Long family of Dunston Hall. I hope he would approve of its present restoration.

# CHAPTER 13

# Operation Arthritis

In April 1978 I had a hip replacement operation, done by the famous orthopaedic surgeon G. K. McKee, the pioneer who developed artificial hip joints at a time when hip surgery was in its infancy. My operation was, and is, entirely successful.

It followed weeks of pain and finally rapid deterioration in mobility. A walk to the end of the garden was my limit. Going upstairs was a major effort.

In 1978 my G.P. told me the waiting list for hip operations on the National Health Service was four to five years. I was seventy-eight. The waiting time for a private operation was six weeks. Cost: £2,000. I was living on a pension. No way could I afford £2,000.

I told Dorothy, who has remained a much loved friend ever since I visited her as a little girl half a century ago in Oriel College, and she said instantly, "I will give you the money."

Such generosity was overwhelming.

I also wrote to my niece in South Africa. A few days later I had a telephone call.

"Won't you let me pay?" she said.

That was Thursday. On Saturday morning her London office rang me to say the money had been paid into my bank account.

Writing this twelve years later still leaves me with a lump

in my throat. No one can ever have such generous friends and relatives as I have.

Six weeks later, lying in hospital after the hip replacement, I wondered what could be done to help people less fortunate. "Going private" had been against all my socialist principles. Yet if I had waited five years in pain and increasing disability, I would have been of little use to the Mental Health Association in which I was still involved, or to the elderly brother who lived with me, or indeed to anyone else. It was a difficult decision to make, and one I felt could only be justified if something practical could be done to help cut the waiting list for others. During that fortnight in hospital I thought of little else.

After a number of fruitless approaches to people and organisations, I got in touch with Arthritis Care and met its president, Sheelin Knollys. She was the first person to give me encouragement and I shall always be indebted to her for it.

Arthritis Care then called a meeting. Its chairman, Dr. Cardoe, at that time in charge of St. Michael's Hospital, Aylsham, suggested that if we could raise money to build a new operating theatre in St. Michael's, more operations could be done than in their existing very small surgical facility.

I then went to the Norfolk Health Authority and was told a new facility would cost £200,000. They confirmed that this would certainly help, though still not eliminate the waiting lists.

The next step was to find a chairman for the project, and we were most fortunate in finding someone who knew Norfolk well and was also a most competent chairman, Jonathan Peel. Sheelin agreed to be vice-chairman, and these two, together with a third supporter, John Steward, formed a working committee and made my dream come true. We called it "Operation Arthritis."

125

Within a year building began. The finished facility was opened by the Duchess of Kent in May 1982. By the time we closed the appeal we had raised over £420,000, and had spent our surplus, after the operating theatre was paid for, on building a new five-bedded ward and updating another.

I have been involved with many money-raising efforts, but never before in one which evoked such widespread enthusiasm. It seemed that everyone had known someone who had waited too long in considerable pain for a hip operation. One donation was from a builder who had waited eight years for a hospital bed. Within three months after his hip replacement he was back on the scaffolding, working normally. He bicycled ten miles to bring his contribution to my door.

Operation Arthritis was given a room by the Health Authority to use as an office and we employed a part-time paid typist for a year. All the fundraisers donated their services, and so did the artists who appeared at the Theatre Royal, Norwich, for our gala benefit performance. For a short time we had advice from a paid professional fundraiser.

It had always been hard to convince the general public that mental health was a charity worth supporting. Not so for Operation Arthritis. Even our busy M.P., John MacGregor, somehow found time to organise two variety shows to boost our funds. Public support was magnificent

Since we built the new facility, many more hip and knee replacements have been provided in Norfolk. Not enough, of course. Nor will there be, till the N.H.S. provides more surgeons.

In my ninetieth year my great niece, Mary Ann Wingfield, wrote to ask me if she could write my biography.

"How absurd!" was my first reaction. Then on second thoughts it seemed more practical to do it myself.

Perhaps younger members of my family might find it amusing to read of a way of life and a cost of living very different from the 1990s. For my part I wonder at their astronomical salaries, their cars, their clothes and their credit cards. But I am glad that at their age I could walk about London by myself without fear of mugging, and that even as a social worker I never met drug addicts. Today's younger generation certainly has problems.

Now, at 93, sitting in the house I resurrected, and turning away from my old-fashioned typewriter, I can look out at my garden I dug and scythed and cleared and planted with the help of friends. Thanks to Mr McKee I can still walk round it.

And thanks to two cataract operations I can watch the woodpecker and the nuthatch on the bird table without glasses. But above all my thanks go to friends and family who have always come to the rescue at times of trouble and made all this possible. I have been fortunate indeed.